FAMILY COURT PERILS

A Real Life Event Exposes Pitfalls
in the
Family Law No-fault Divorce Process

RACHEL MADDOX

Preface

_I_ write this book, not just because the subject matter is of professional interest to me as a social scientist, but also because to ignore evil is itself evil. That means there was moral pressure on me to write this book. The shocking revelations on flawed human character and a judicial system open to selfish exploitation, have motivated me to slip my professional anxieties about institutionalised unfairness between the covers of this book. It is noteworthy that goddess Justitia, the allegorical Roman personification of justice depicted on the front cover of this book, is not completely blindfolded nor are the scales in her hand evenly balanced – a symbolic indication of what to expect.

In writing this book, professional detachment is a key consideration. That means my personal opinion is not important. Evaluation of behaviours and outcomes in this narrative is based on standards that come from social values and norms or from principles in relevant disciplines of the social sciences. The disciplines most relevant are law, psychology, sociology, and political science. Matters outside my area of expertise are raised as questions, specifically on deeper questions of law requiring a pantheon of legal wisdom.

This book could not have been written without help. I am most grateful to those who were kind enough to provide it. But it is not possible to acknowledge everyone who contributed to the wide learning that this book embodies, given its multi-disciplinary nature. The narrative explains the investigated case by treating it as a human problem, rather than as just a legal problem, in order to get to the bottom of what really happened. The fields of Hypergamy, Sociopathy, and mercenary syndrome are sources of perceptual depth. A social sciences perspective subsumes the legal to be able to see the forest and not just the trees – that is, for fuller understanding. Coming to grips with a multifaceted phenomenon requires a multidimensional approach for a panoptic frame of reference.

The essential features of the narrative are believed to be based on verifiable material facts that are considered accurate and sacrosanct. They are presented in good faith and with a social purpose. The central issue is not who won, but whether justice was served. In the unfolding narrative objective analysis is applied to extract a social message from a life event – leading to the identification of desperately needed judicial reforms in the final chapter.

However, for the sake of completeness, some dots needed to be joined. That was done on the basis of informed judgement and ballpark conjecture. But using beliefs to fill in blanks here and there on incidental personal matters to achieve coherence does not detract from critical aspects of the analysis directly pertaining to social justice. Such aspects are presumed to be factual and verifiable. The blank-filling aspects are elaborative additions that are only ornamental, and not therefore relevant and consequential to the essence of the narrative and the validity of the evaluation. The facts material to the legal case are thus sound and intact. Emphatically, the filler aspects do not downgrade the professional integrity that underpins the heart of the message on court systems pervading the book.

The lightened expression in the book, it is hoped, will enhance the readability of its content without reducing accuracy or seriousness. The idea is to remove the cloak of mystery shrouding the Family Law divorce process in the Family Court system, and make poignant explanation as jargon-free as possible. I hope this book contributes in some small way towards removing heartbreaking inequities in the judicial processes for family separation.

I am grateful for the unstinting support and love of those who encouraged me to persevere and the others who took the time and trouble to give me feedback on different aspects of the manuscript. A special thanks to my life-long friends, analyst Bernard Anthonisz and his lawyer son Michael, for the latter. Last, but not least, I express my deep gratitude to Leanne Gruber, Professor of Psychology, for the countless discussions and insightful suggestions on the behavioural idiosyncrasies manifested by central players in this case.
The Author
October 2019

Table of Contents

TABLE OF CONTENTS

AUTOPSIC EVALUATION: DIRE FINDINGS

CONCLUSION: LOST CAUSE?

***

Chapter 1
INTRODUCTION: SETTING THE TONE

"There, but for the grace of God, go I"
John Bunyan (1628-88) author of 'Pilgrims Progress'

1.1 Scope of Narrative

In this book facts are used to question faith in judicial processes. The hard facts of a true story about a relationship breakdown are used to dispute prevailing common beliefs about how the Family Court system for separation actually operates. The idea is to use the individual life event to draw out a broad message for everybody. That includes information on the interplay between personality symptoms and judicial systems.

There was to be a brand new approach to family separation. The Family Law Act 1975 was hailed as a progressive law reform featuring as its centrepiece 'no-fault' divorce that revolutionised the divorce law in Australia. The Family Law Act removed 'fault' as a ground for divorce and replaced it with 'irretrievable breakdown.' That innovation promised to reduce conflict from antagonistic partners trying to find fault with each other, thereby enabling a friendlier or less bitter separation process.

The 'no-fault' basis was to be the beating heart of an innovative Family Court system. The spanking piece of legal architecture enshrined hopes of a process that was simple, flexible, and cheap, all happening within a court system with a heart. The dedicated court system swept the public off its feet with a promise of friendliness. 'Caring' was to be a key defining trait of the specialised Family Court system.

But the reality is different. The Family Court system has drifted a long way from the noble intentions of its founders. As a result, the 'no-fault' basis has lost much of its envisioned sparkle. The information in *Family Court Perils* is expected to throw light on where things have reached and why. The assessment is to be based on a real life narrative that speaks to the state of the Family Court system by illustrating lurking perils that bedevil it.

That tale is grounded in fact. Importantly, the tale is not intended to be anti-female or anti-male – just anti-unfairness as backed by sturdy facts. The facts of life in the unfolding story are left to speak for themselves and the resulting chips left to fall where they may. They warn of a family separation process that is better approached with uneasy disquiet than self-assured optimism. This concern is backed by academic historian John Hirst, who in *Quarterly Essay*, labels the Family Court a "Kangaroo Court" (Hirst 2005, p1) – a colourful but uncomplimentary description meaning a crude court that ignores or perverts recognised standards of law and justice. An extreme interpretation is when the label applies to a mock court characterised by dishonesty and incompetence.

1.2 Nature of Narrative

The picture to be painted will require a big canvas and bold brushwork. While this narrative hangs on a framework of verifiable material facts, the picture painted is big because it is broader than the legal. Key social, cultural, ethical, psychological, and institutional aspects are interwoven into the legal and join dots for greater meaningfulness in an unfolding story. Hard facts are presented within a wider context of explanation for better understanding of the multifaceted human condition. Figuring prominently in making sense of the qualities behind observed player behaviour are the to-be explained conditions of hypergamy, Sociopathy, and mercenary – aspects that guard against losing the thread in what is an interwoven narrative. All commentary on the described events is designed to tease out or emphasize key points relevant to the yardstick of fair play.

The process is the focus. In building the narrative, the focus is on the judicial procedures that need to be navigated for family separation. Dysfunction in judicial processes implies the existence of deeply ingrained systemic vulnerabilities for most disputants. The striking incidents in this story pull back the curtain to reveal the abysmal gap between hoped-for fairness and the disappointing reality.

Demystification is the idea. That happens by providing a rare insight into how the wheels of justice creakingly turned in response to the application of the Family Law to an unfolding relationship breakdown. We go behind the scenes, to the innards of the judicial process, to uncover the mysterious nuts and bolts of court mechanisms for the uninitiated.

That helps because: forewarned is forearmed. As amazing as it may seem to the trusting, court processes meant for good can be used for ill, to deny them the assumed ring of plausibility. This narrative describes a worst-case scenario and flashes alarm signals at the many harrowing perils that can really occur while achingly journeying through a shadowy judicial channel. The pinpointed horrors have the capability to cumulatively reverberate and rattle confidence in fair play.

In addition, this narrative highlights incremental developments leading to, and associated with, the climax of a baffling court outcome. That means this narrative can identify possibilities that are unlikely to be fondly remembered.

Judicial reform is the end objective of these endeavours. Getting to the bottom of things through deep-lying explanations will enable the focus of this discourse to evolve from present fumble to future solution. It is hoped the suggested innovation will do much to reinvigorate the 'no-fault' beating heart of a caring Family Court system. The future in store can be an improvement on the apparatus in place.

That hopefully explains the tone and scope of this presentation, with the tone intended to be thoughtful and the scope intended to be broad.

1.3 Primary Players

Identities do not matter because behaviours shape this narrative. *Family Court Perils* is not about individuals *per se*, but about their conduct in relation to court process. The personal experiences are used to elicit a social message in relation to just and honourable treatment, action, and outcomes. For that reason it is not necessary to identify individuals in order to fulfil the objectives of this book. Pseudonyms serve to disguise the identities of all players in the drama, namely disputants, attorneys, and court officials. Also hidden are specific dates and places.

Nevertheless, several villains are revealed. Since baddies do not display reptilian tails, they are recognised by their disagreeable behaviours. The primary focus is on showing the smorgasbord of unethical, illegal, and inept conduct of litigants, lawyers, and other court players that is facilitated by court processes open to abuse without any sort of penalty. Also exposed are the perils of the pre-trial process, the centrepiece of the Family Court system, and its overwhelming ability to unpleasantly surprise.

Playing a lead role in the drama is the wife, to whom we give the fictitious name Mary. Mary is a migrant from an Asian country, brought over to Australia by her Australian husband for the purpose of marriage 20 years before the separation. She was a widow aged 52 at the time and her Australian husband, referred to as Shaun, was then aged 56. There occurred a dual benefit to Mary, as by marrying Shaun she was able to join her immediate family of six members from an earlier marriage already resident in Sydney at the time. Mary was the matriarch of a close-knit family, which came to have 12 immediate adult members at the time of separation. That there was close interaction among family members is a fact of importance to future harsh developments in the case.

Mary's youngest offspring of her previous marriage, a son given the false name Ashley, was the black sheep of the family. He has a catalytic influence in the story to be told. Ashley could not make it into university, had undertaken some sort of minimal vocational course, was only sporadically employed and hence often dependent on social welfare. Mary's eldest son, assigned the false name Ian, was the artful mastermind behind the ruthless divorce strategy that pushed moral and legal boundaries to uncover gaping pitfalls in the judicial system. His bad antics are put to good purpose when they energise this story with the unimaginable.

Husband Shaun was a professional, and featured in Australia's *Who's Who* by the time he married Mary. For 12 years before retirement during his marriage to Mary, he travelled twice a month for most months to all parts of the world on consultancies, the work also taking him to parts of Asia where shopping was cheap. Mary accompanied him on most trips, using the occasions to sightsee and shop for herself and the grandchildren. This information is relevant to the case to come, because Mary had no income in Australia, and all her living expenses, including travel and shopping expenses, were met by her husband. It later transpired that under Family Court 'no-fault' practices, such provider generosity was, paradoxically, a settlement liability.

Husband Shaun divorced his previous wife to marry Mary. A matter to note is that husband Shaun had one child from his previous marriage, to whom we give the name Matthew. Matthew was mentally disabled and partially dependant on Shaun. This matter is of major significance in the story to come, but turned out in the end to be of no relevance to the 'no-fault' Family Court.

1.4 The Court Process

For the Family Court system, the ideal has proven to be too utopian. The process that exists has moved a long way from the noble ideals of its founders, which included enabling couples to part without trauma and expense. In reality, the process is anything but friendly and cheap.

The Family Court process is scarred by an adversarial system and marred by process laxity. It will be shown to provide fertile ground for unethical, militant, and slipshod practices. It is ruthlessly oppositional, being riddled with belligerency, even though the Family Law Act removed finding fault as a ground for divorce.

While the focus of this narrative is on the Family Court, with Family Law governing that main game, a criminal element can often sneak in as a subordinate event. Those going to the Family Court for divorce settlement in Australia can find themselves also going to another court, namely a Local Court, to make the welcome or unwelcome acquaintance of a magistrate. That is because the Family

Law for separation provides strong pointed incentives for a two-pronged strategy to enable greater success in terms of financial gain and child custody. The badly treated party in the family relationship would have a stronger case if they can first prove maltreatment in the Local Court – success in the Local Court resonating as a settlement boost in the Family Court.

It is an open secret that process abuse is not confined to disputants. Hence it is hard to overlook an old favourite: lawyers. It will be revealed that the system as it operates places principled lawyers at a disadvantage when up against cunning opposition. What happened will show that some lawyers ungrudgingly contribute to the unfairness of the process by ducking procedural requirements and ignoring their professional call to justness. Subscribing to the Family Court's caring mission is not among every family lawyer's aspirations.

For these reasons, the Family Court process unsurprisingly changes behaviour. The behaviours of all the players will be fashioned by a Court that spawns a culture of hostility, the polarisation from which has a ghastly reputation of turning love into hate and making enemies of friends. Apart from the disputants, also adversely swayed are the behaviours of lawyers and court officials, particularly registrars. Registrars, though being weighty players in Family Court proceedings, are shown to have the potential to be the soft underbelly of the entire Family Court system. To once again quote John Hirst in *Kangaroo Court*: "One of the gravest failings of the Family Court derives from the noble intentions of its founders" (Hirst 2005 p1).

It is a peculiar Court because trials are rare. The information to be presented will throw light on the true nature of the apparatus in play, specifically why less than ten percent of cases in the Family Court system reach trial. The overwhelming majority of cases are resolved through conciliation, or agreement between the parties and their lawyers, at the level of the registrar. This behavioural result is not necessarily because things are fine in the Family Court system – far from it. It happens because of something chronically deep-seated and worryingly sinister. This narrative will colourfully disclose what they are.

Dishonesty surfaces as the better policy. This analysis will highlight how and why, because of the way in which the system operates, deceitfulness can be rewarded at the expense of integrity, greed at the expense of bigheartedness, and evil at the cost of love. That can make expectation of fairness a cruel hoax.

Having revealed the drift in the plot, we proceed to the pivotal point in the real life experience giving underpinning relevance to the analytic content of the narrative. Presented next is the beginning of an unfolding series of events that feature in the dramatic tale of the investigated relationship breakdown.

***

Chapter 2

TWO BOMBSHELLS: SHOW ME THE MONEY

2.1 Beginning of the End

It was a bolt from the blue. There was a momentous development at 7.40am on 18 October when dark clouds suddenly overhung a marriage. They replaced the blue skies present just a moment before. It was when, after some 20 years into what husband Shaun believed was a generally happy marriage, he was informed by wife Mary over morning coffee in bed that she wanted to separate. There was no pussyfooting when she sternly demanded that he purchase for her a separate apartment. Mary's firm pronouncement was to trigger a major life crisis for both. But for now, while Shaun's outlook became suddenly cloudy, Mary's was crystal clear.

Mary was carrying out a scheme hatched over many months with eldest son Ian. Shaun had no idea that wife Mary was in the process of implementing a calculated plan to leave him. Mary's cold decision to induce the separation meant for Shaun there was 'trouble in paradise.' He was pushed into uncharted waters where life as he had known it for 20 years would fall apart at age 76.

Being dumped was hard to believe. At first Shaun did not take his wife seriously. But hers was not a passing thought. Mary's demand to separate and get her a place came as a surprise to Shaun, even though there had been some tension in the relationship on 26

February of that year. That was when Shaun protested recently discovered hidden excess baggage Mary harboured in the marriage. Mary was told by Shaun she should stop secretly channelling large amounts of household retirement income to fund the extravagant lifestyle of her then 36 year old married son Ashley, the youngest offspring of her previous marriage.

Much more on this weighty matter will be presented in Chapter 4. Suffice to know for now that Mary had agreed to stop the payments after consulting eldest son Ian, and life resumed as normal on the surface. It included prolonged overseas travel from late May to mid-September that featured an upmarket Rhine river cruise, as well as stays, coach tours and train trips in the UK, Continental Europe, and Asia. Overseas visits lasting months at a time had been a feature of their lifestyle since Shaun retired nine years ago.

Mary's eldest son Ian was more than a proactive accomplice. Ian was reflexively complicit in aiding and abetting all his mother's desires throughout her marriage to Shaun. That included the systematic exploitation of the marriage by facilitating the stealthy flow of significant household money to his brother Ashley, in which activity his wife was a secret enabler. He had a substantial input into crafting his mother's court testimony, as later explained. He had no pangs of conscience about backing his mother's falsehoods with congruent fiery hearsay untruths of the inadmissible sort (that are later shown to have got nowhere). His mother's divorce case was a culmination; risking a blot on his biography, he chose to be the inglorious architect of all aspects of the unprincipled strategy that was mercilessly pursued in this case.

The rare 26 February conflict between the couple had uneven effects. While it lingered as an unsettling memory for Shaun, it was a call to arms for Mary. Mary was unhappy because old habits die hard; she had difficulty coping with the fact that her regular support payments to son Ashley had ceased after decades. She discussed with son Ian how to restore the lost support which Ashley had come to depend upon for many years, especially now that his wife was pregnant with their first child. Mother and son Ian decided the only way to ensure Ashley's future was by separating from Shaun – and simultaneously separating Shaun from his life's savings.

Ashley's gravy train was temporarily sidelined. Although his income slumped when his extrinsic largesse ceased, Mary came to regard the forgone money transfers to Ashley as being only an interim measure to buy time. It was to be short-term till the grand move to separate from Shaun could be secretly planned with the counsel of a lawyer friend, we name Mr. Crack.

The settlement was to be informal. Mary emphasised she did not want the hassle of a legal case. The separation should be amicable, she said; they could still be friends and meet up from time to time while leading separate lives. It was a case of: 'just give me the money and things will be fine.' She felt she was being kind to Shaun, giving him an easy way out, knowing full well the strong-arm options up her sleeve. In her view her words were merciful, but with the undertone of a threatening 'cough up or else.' She was to later walk the talk by going to the police and using severe measures, then held in reserve, to deadly effect.

But at the time Mary did not think it would come to that. She was confident she could successfully skirt the formal legal process because of two reasons. Firstly, Shaun had a known abhorrence of legal action; he saw it as an unedifying experience that involved the expensive locking of horns for a hate-filled slugfest. Secondly, Mary held in reserve a secret strategy devised by lawyer friend Mr Crack. He was the architect of what was considered to be a sure-fire, albeit diabolical, standby plan (shortly revealed) to ensure Mary got what she wanted without a court case.

Mary stood firm. She displayed a rare streak of unrelenting determination to separate despite pleadings from Shaun to let bygones be bygones. Although Mary maintained an unwavering stance on wanting to separate, the couple continued to go out together, including seeing the musical play 'Aladdin', to two house parties, and several private lunches and coffees. Shaun kept hoping she would change her mind. This information will have considerable significance in assessing subsequent unexpectedly severe developments in the case

2.2 Point of No Return

Unbeknown to Shaun, Mary had burned her boats. Mary's unyielding demand to separate, and rejection of Shaun's pleas that she not do so, is explained by the fact that she had taken an irrevocable step. Pulling rank, matriarch Mary firmly announced to her immediate family of 12 adults, who had a loving relationship with Shaun for some 20 years, she was leaving him. She was doing so because of 20 years of domestic violence, his having an overseas mistress for 12 years, and severe financial abuse.

For the family, a state of shock followed their initial astonishment. How on earth could there have been such a dark secret when they were in such close touch and had spent prolonged periods together over the many years? The ratbag image of Shaun now portrayed by Mary was starkly contrary to that of the upright 'papa' the grandchildren and others knew, loved, and respected. Mary later formally confirmed that her family knew nothing about the ongoing violence, mistress, and financial abuse, until she informed them for the first time ever on that pivotal day, 18 October.

Poisoning the family against Shaun was crucial to Mary's objective. Manipulation was essential to pry loose from the family someone who was integral to it; she had to condemn Shaun to justify leaving him without legal action. That is what psychologists call 'Family Alienation Syndrome.' Apart from her eldest son Ian and his wife, none of the others knew about the financial milking for son Ashley that had been quietly taking place for years. Shaun was completely in the dark about what Mary had told her family he had supposedly done. He was shattered when he came to know about it several weeks later, as it was completely untrue.

Matriarch Mary's game plan was working perfectly. She was pleased the offensive information she told her family about Shaun's alleged bad behaviour had succeeded in turning against him the family he had grown to love and come to regard as his own. Those family members having niggling doubts about Mary's allegations against Shaun nevertheless closed ranks behind her for the reasons to be shortly explained. Mary told Shaun he was not to contact any member on her side of the family, thereby isolating him. It was a turning point in Shaun's life, as the rift created was an unbridgeable chasm. He lost the only family he knew and was to forever thereafter plough a lonely furrow.

A mutually reinforcing combination of cultural compulsions and power relationships explains the family alienation. Mary hailed from an Asian collectivistic culture where group interest transcends individual interest. That means family ties demand tribal loyalty, the ties binding sufficient to cause commitment to family to supersede commitment to Shaun. But intra-family power relationships, based on rank from seniority, were additional intrinsic factors explaining the unified family stance. Mary's eldest son Ian used his seniority to peddle her concoctions to which he was party. Ostracism from openly disagreeing with matriarch Mary and eldest son Ian was simply too high a penalty for sceptical family members.

But Mary was trapped. Short term gain came at the risk of long term problems. While her strategy served its purpose at the time, it meant Mary had painted herself into a corner by the untruths she had told her family about Shaun. Her family network gave her strength from unity relative to Shaun, who had no-one. She could not allow the truth be known as that would mean family support lost. Family backing was crucial for the battle ahead; the damaging allegations she had made had to somehow be sustained. She had dug a hole for herself and had no plausible way of climbing out. Only continued demonization of Shaun would enable Mary to keep averting the backfire from a crisis of credibility with her family. As later explained, a police complaint helped her to do just that; among other things, it was meant to substantiate her assertions against Shaun and thereby buttress her position within her wide family circle.

2.3 Measured Pressure

The family home was to be lost. Shaun informed Mary that to buy her a separate place, the apartment that was their beautiful and comfortably customised home, would need to be sold, the mortgage paid, and the balance proceeds amounting to about $500K used to make the purchase she wanted. The equity in the apartment was from Shaun's superannuation savings and, since the apartment had previously been his investment property, was in his sole name. This last point later turned out to be significant, as failing to take Shaun's sole ownership status into account derailed Mary's deadly reserve strategy and seriously complicated the case, as will soon become apparent.

The road ahead was to be painfully tortuous. For now Mary was secure in the belief that Shaun wanted to do the best he could to avoid legal action; she knew he had a sense of déjà vu about court action being a Pandora's Box of turmoil and expense. Mary did not know at the time that her unfair demand upon the sale of the property was going to give Shaun no choice but to reluctantly start the ball rolling on legal action, that the process would take a horror-filled 16 months, and financially ruin him in the end.

Unaware of the perils ahead, Shaun did what was necessary for an amicable parting. He researched the Internet and found two apartments in retirement villages close to Mary's family for her to inspect so she could pick one to purchase in her name. He drove her to each place, so she could consider the pros and cons of each. Mary insisted on having her family also inspect both apartments on a different occasion, and this happened. Mary preferred one of the two at a price of $220K, and title documents were arranged. This was satisfactory to Shaun as it meant that if he gave her $30K in cash they would each have half share of the assets in the pool and a bitter court case and high legal costs would be avoided. Shaun was perplexed when Mary cast aside in rejection the title documents he gave her – foreshadowing the trouble to come.

Shaun proceeded to undertake the legal necessities. As the family home was in Shaun's sole name, it was he who had to find the real estate agent and sign the sales agreement. Mary cooperated with the sale process, keeping the kitchen tidy, putting flowers in the vase, and standing outside with Shaun during public inspection times.

The home property sold in three weeks. Shaun accepted the first purchase offer close to the advertised price. He thereafter informed Mary of the sale and its price.

2.4 Spoke in Wheel

Unexpectedly, Shaun's action displeased Mary. Shaun was surprised when his logical action of agreeing to sell, considered harmless, caused quite a stir. Mary was annoyed the sale had been finalised without her knowledge, even though it was close to the advertised price. She and son Ian had been denied the option of rejecting it. The duo had to do something about that perceived insult. This was the thin edge of a massive wedge, as it later resulted in unexpected dastardly developments that turned the tables on Shaun.

For a start, something Shaun never dreamed of happened out of the blue. He was shocked to receive a call from the real estate agent managing the sale to say that Mary and son Ian had dropped by in an attempt to stop the sale. The estate agent had declined to discuss the matter of the sale with them because Shaun had sole ownership and was the sole party to the contract of sale. Mary and Ian were told they had no status in the matter. They stormed off in a huff. Humiliated and confused they went to Ian's place to plot their next move. What they decided in consultation with their lawyer friend Mr. Crack was a shocker. The crisis deepened.

But first, let us note two implications of Mary's actions.

For one thing, it was puzzling to Shaun as to why the sale was to be stopped. It was even more puzzling when several weeks later he came to know of Mary's awful allegations of violence against him to her family. If Mary's assertions of violence were to hold water, surely selling the family home was a 'get-out-of-jail-card' for someone truly suffering loathsome domestic violence as claimed by Mary? So trying to stop the sale was behaviour inconsistent with wanting to hurriedly escape the allegedly repulsive domestic situation.

For another, there was in their action an unexpected overtone of anger barely masked. By going behind Shaun's back Mary and son had crossed the Rubicon. That was a defining moment for the couple; good faith crumpled even though Shaun and Mary continued to share the same bed after the incident for several weeks thereafter. From then on a cordial relationship became strained, the relationship dipping to new low ebb. The potential for conflict ominously hovered.

Shaun chose to ignore what he knew. He did not question Mary about her visit to the property agent when she came home that evening, an angry Mary opening the front door with uncharacteristic forcefulness. Shaun had to help when the key jammed.

Shaun was greatly troubled. The spectre of legal action loomed. Mary's sudden uptick in aggression contributed much to Shaun's fading hopes of an amicable settlement. Shaun's destiny was uncertain while Mary's moves, based on her secret plan, gave her a heady confidence. But she was careful not to telegraph her punches. She held back what more she had to say till a few days later. She knew that what she had to say would cause the currently simmering tension to assume menacing proportions.

2.5 Paper Roses

A second bombshell was to explode a few days later. What Mary said then caused matters, already grim for Shaun, to take a startling turn for the worse. Over coffee in bed a few mornings later, Mary revealed the diabolical plan given to her by her lawyer friend, Mr. Crack. It was to Mary the cat's meow. Mary told Shaun she would not be leaving the already sold premises to give vacant possession to the new owner unless she received, not 50 percent, but 70 percent of the net proceeds of sale from the property.

The greedy demand freaked out Shaun. He found it shockingly offensive that the relationship he thought was based on love had crudely defaulted to money. He felt a chill running through him; it was a sobering moment of truth.

Realization dawned. Shaun suddenly recognised he had been in a fool's paradise till then because of what psychologists refer to as 'Cognitive Dissonance' – a theory propounded by leading psychologist Leon Festinger in his 1957 book *A Theory of Cognitive Dissonance*. Cognitive dissonance causes people to modify their thoughts and behaviours so as to accommodate unpleasant situations and thereby reduce tension in relationships. That can be interpreted to mean that people get along better when they are in a state of denial about warning signs in the relationship, or carry on by rationalising such red flags in the relationship.

Turning a blind eye had been convenient. In this instance, cognitive dissonance came from the clash between what Shaun subconsciously knew what Mary was up to and his carrying on of normal life with her in spite of it. But the second bombshell was an eye-opener. Now for the first time ever the reality of what Mary was really like reached unacceptable proportions. Shaun was finally hit by the utterly shocking realization that Mary was a wolf in sheep's clothing he had to get away from, however gut-wrenching the process.

Mary had the solid backing of son Ian in adopting such a highhanded position. He was backstop for unprincipled behaviour Shaun had never imagined would happen. Refusing Mary's demand for 70/30 brought Shaun nothing but trouble. It was the harbinger of excruciating future misery

However, Mary and son Ian considered their heightened demand to be fully justified. They wanted to teach Shaun a lesson for his cockiness in not consulting Mary before he concluded the property sale, and also because they could not stop the sale about which she had not been consulted. Mary wanted the sale terminated because she wanted to carry on with Shaun as before. Her change of heart about the sale resulted from a realisation that 50 percent of the pool of assets was too small to justify abandoning her five-star lifestyle. Only 70 percent, rather than half-share, would make leaving worthwhile because the money had to be enough for *both* her and failed son Ashley. Mary did not realise her magnified demand put her out on a on a legal limb and would spark a legal conflagration.

Shaun's pleadings were to no avail. Time and time again Shaun appealed to Mary to settle for 50/50, but Mary's wanting to support Ashley made her impervious to his reasoning. Shaun explained to

Mary the plight both he and his partially dependent son would be in if he met her unreasonable demand for 70 percent. It was a forlorn hope because 70/30 had become a Holy Grail for Mary and a spanner in the works for Shaun. Mary was unmoved because it was all Shaun's fault. Shaun had brought the elevated 70 percent demand upon himself. She salved her conscience by blaming Shaun for selling the property from beneath her. So pay up he must.

There was method to her apparent madness; Mary knew exactly what she was doing. She confidently stood her ground because she was, after all, a member of an artful triumvirate together with son Ian and lawyer Mr. Crack. Mary had never been demanding before; her inner demons were exhibited for the first time in 20 years. Her less-than charming conduct may seem like bad and 'faulty' behaviour to ordinary folk with even a dash of human decency. But that was not a problem. Mary was assured by lawyer friend Mr. Crack that her morally questionable *modus operandi* was perfectly legal under the indulgent 'no-fault' provision of the Family Law Act.

Mary's behaviour throws up significant insight on the effect of the Family Law Act on everyday living. Open family conflict is unnecessary for the 'no-fault' provision of the Family Law Act to become operational. The 'no-fault' provision of the Family Law Act, by its mere jurisdictional presence, is capable of reaching inside family homes, to influence the behaviour of empowered parties for good or ill in all ongoing family relationships. Recognition of this reality provides an early foretaste of worse to come.

Shaun was trapped. Shaun realised it was the last gasp for his hope of an easy separation. As bad as things were for Shaun, it was child's play compared to what Mary and eldest son Ian had in store for him.

2.6 Enter Lawyers

Uncertainty beckoned. Alarmed, a frantic Shaun rushed to see a lawyer in Sydney city the next day. Shaun was caught between the proverbial devil and the deep blue sea. On the one hand, he faced the unacceptable choice of agreeing to Mary's refusal to vacate. That would bring dire legal consequences from breach of the sales contract. On the other hand, he faced the unacceptable choice of giving in to Mary's demand (something she was counting on). If he conceded Mary's unfair demand for 70/30 to vacate, he and disabled son Matthew would be in financial difficulty. He could never buy himself a retirement place with just 30 percent of the asset pool, and since he had a dependant disabled son Mathew, whose property he had a legal obligation to maintain for the rest of Matthew's life, Mathew would face homelessness (an important point elaborated on in Chapter 9).

Shaun's legal action was to backfire on him. Although Shaun regarded his legal action as a defensive measure to save himself and his son, Mary saw the legal action as an attack on herself and her son. They had no qualms about using the juggernaut of that very legal system to bulldoze or crush him. It is clear that whilst it was Shaun who initiated the case, his proactive and hostile 'Applicant' court status (that made Mary 'Respondent'), had been thrust upon him. His earlier measured actions in trying to resolve the separation amicably to avoid court action attests to that. Sucked into the vile vortex of court action against his will, the initiation of legal proceedings against wife Mary was to have devastating repercussions on his life and financial future. Shaun had sowed the wind and was to reap the whirlwind.

Shaun knew that the first meeting with his Family Law solicitor, whom we name Gianna, was the beginning of a painful long haul. But he never knew how painful and how long the ordeal would be. Following Shaun's emergency consultation with Gianna, the following developments took place.

Shaun abandoned his solely-owned home. On Gianna's legal advice, Shaun hurriedly left his now-sold family home for alternative rental accommodation on Christmas Eve. That was over two months since Mary's announcement of wanting to separate. In a weak moment, when Mary saw him silently packing, she told him there was no need to leave. She did not know legal action was in train, and that Shaun could not possibly continue to live there while that was happening. Shaun was painfully aware that the forthcoming adversarial court process had the gruesome ability to turn Mary's current indifference into future enmity.

Rental accommodation imposed enduring financial hardship on Shaun. Moving in was not a shoo-in in the competitive rental market. Shaun was spooked by gloom when he discovered that no-one would rent to him without a landlord reference or employment income. In desperation he took out a cash advance on his credit card to pay an advance of six month's rent on a six month contract to stand a chance in the tight rental market. He thought he could pay it off from the expected house sale proceeds. But a later Family Court decision prevented that and caused the loan to be an albatross around his neck that severely hamstrung his lifestyle.

In a last ditch attempt to save his marriage, Shaun invited Mary to accompany him to his new place of abode until they could find a suitable retirement apartment together. The request was met with stony silence. But the request was redundant as Mary had already spoken some days earlier. When some days before Shaun was to leave he pleaded with Mary not to leave him she had said: "Just wanting me is not enough."

Shaun's life was in turmoil. He had no amicable shots left in his locker. He was all alone at 76 years of age facing the suspense of trouble and strife. Besides the sadness of wrenching separation from someone he loved, and having to bear the stress of providing copious information to his lawyer for the legal action he had just started, he had other abnormal tasks to accomplish. He needed to find removalists at short notice, pack his clothing and take what minimal furniture he could fit into a studio apartment, get new electricity, phone, and TV connections while not discontinuing these in the place he was leaving, clean both places, stock his larder – and all the rest of it.

Immediate settlement was offered. Shaun wanted the matter over with. After Shaun's traumatic departure from the family home, a letter was issued by Shaun's lawyer Gianna to Mary four days later on 28 December requiring Mary to vacate the sold apartment she was forcibly occupying within three weeks on the payment of $20K. An offer of final settlement at 50 percent of the net assets in the pool was made at the same time.

Mary played hardball. Both offers were rejected by a lawyer Mary had engaged on legal aid. While Mary's lawyer might have had an interest in dragging things on to line his pockets, there was happy happenstance from Mary's perseverance for settlement at 70/30. Hope of early settlement was dashed. Mary and her legal aid lawyer skipped the bit about the speedy settlement offer at 50 percent. That had struck a discordant note with Mary and eldest son Ian, who saw it as steamrollering them into taking a loss of 20 percent. They were ready to hunker down for as long as it took until they got the money they had set their sights on. Accepting settlement at 50/50 would have ended the case within a month of filing and saved over $90K in combined legal costs, not to mention the severe stress on the elderly and ailing from a nightmarish 16 months.

If one pauses to take stock, two matters stand out. Firstly, while Shaun's lawyer's primary role was that of a shield for defence, Mary's lawyer had the primary role of a weapon for attack. Subsequent developments were to automatically degenerate the offensive-defensive relationship to that of predator-prey. Second, if things had been different, and the Family Court had operated according to its original mission of providing quick and inexpensive solutions, perhaps matters could have been settled then and there.

Current Family Court procedures let Mary call the shots. She was fixated on getting 70 percent of the net assets by including in the settlement pool the value of disabled stepson Matthew's property, now transferred free-of-charge to the Government under the Social Security Act 1991. It was a property that Shaun was still legally responsible for maintaining despite the absence of rental income from it. This property was a bugbear that was to make the difference between victory and defeat in the final settlement. In psychological terms, Mary had an emotional attachment to this objective that subsequent events will show was of a pathological nature. There is an awful lot more to say on this, but that will have to wait.

Let us note for now there was a tripartite barrier to amicable settlement. Shaun's predicament was defined by Mary's determination for settlement at 70 percent of the net pool of assets available, her formal rejection of the offer made for immediate settlement at 50/50, and her refusal to vacate the already sold property despite an advance payment of $20K. Breaking through the barrier exposed Shaun to a slippery slope that led over several months to financial catastrophe for him.

2.7 Unwelcome Boomerang

Force was a last resort. Shaun had no choice but to reluctantly reach for the only practical tool in the box (hardly a thing of beauty): a Family Court Order to eject Mary from the sold property. Only such a horrific move would prevent breach of the sales contract and its attendant dire legal consequences for him. Accordingly, court action was filed and papers served on 10 January notifying Mary of the intention to eject her from the promises.

The serving of the Family Court papers threatening ejection was a transformative red rag to Mary and son Ian. It was a watershed day of reckoning for both parties. Mary's blind faith in a dodgy lawyer had led to a manic intention to stay put in the forcibly occupied apartment until the money she wanted dropped in her lap. Mary had placed all her eggs in the 'blackmail' basket on the basis of lawyer Mr. Crack's dubious advice. She had been made to believe that since the property had been sold, Shaun had no choice but to cough up 70 percent of the assets. Astonishingly, they failed to take into account Shaun's sole ownership status that placed Mary in a legally unprotected position. The prospect of a court case was never envisaged. Receiving the Court papers was therefore quite a shocking experience. Lawyer Mr. Crack's devious ploy, of a primrose path to easy money outside the due process of Family Law, was exposed as wishful thinking by the serving of the 'ejection papers.'

Mary was overcome by a mixture of fear and fury. She was hit by a reality that shattered her flight of fantasy on inviolate entitlement; she feared she had lost her grip on Shaun's assets. The way forward, that had been crystal clear to her up to now, suddenly became a bothersome unknown.

Mary's slow burn of anger turned into a bonfire. She was consumed with fury because she was to be thrown out of her home to which she had entitlement as a wife, she believed. Contributing to her frenzy was the fact that her fervent hope for a court-free settlement was now dashed. Mary and eldest son Ian regarded the serving of the Family Court papers threatening ejection as an optional act of aggression by Shaun, blind to the alternative viewpoint that they had been hoist with their own petard. That meant Shaun's legal action, although compelled by necessity, was interpreted by them as an exercise in choice that was mean and arrogant.

Things turned uglier: such supposition was a *casus belli* for Mary and son Ian. It provoked them into lashing out. The last remaining glue of friendship between Shaun and Mary dissolved. That brought new phenomena into play – and they emerged from a can of worms.

All hell broke loose. The court action to force Mary to vacate the sold property was to galvanise vengeance beyond Shaun's wildest nightmares. It triggered a flurry of wild swings at Shaun that cumulatively erupted from then on to give him hell. Legal processes were abused with ruthless ferocity and astonishing impunity to inflict unimaginable harm upon him. There was the devil to pay.

***

Chapter 3

LEGAL VORTEX: PLUNGE INTO UNCERTAINTY

3.1 Here We Go

L egal action was a leap into darkness. Taking the plunge into the lawsuit resulted in a fearsome whirlpool of uncertainty for both parties. It was a scary place to be that they both had sought to avoid. Each party blamed the other for bringing on the anxiety.

A congested court system cut things fine. It was worrying to Shaun that the Family Court Interim Hearing for Mary's ejection was scheduled for as late as 30 January. Since the scheduled date of the property settlement was 6 February, there was a gap of only a week. Mary had to be given time to vacate and Shaun needed time to prepare the apartment for handing over to the buyer in a spotless condition. Also, if Mary ignored the court order to vacate by digging in her heels, further legal action would need to be taken to physically remove her – thereby threatening the property settlement deadline, apart from causing Shaun anguish from having to do such a dreadful thing.

But Mary was not taking things lying down. She was far from amused when her new legal aid lawyer told her she had no choice but to agree to vacate. Mary did not like it one bit as the embarrassment from loss of face was intolerable. She had to do something about it, and in that regard she did not disappoint, as will be shortly disclosed. Because of that secret agenda, it was a far from meek Mary who strode into the Family Court on 30 January.

Ejection did not come cheap. The cost to Shaun of taking the action to make Mary vacate the premises was $15K. Perhaps he would be reimbursed? Let us see.

The strategy had backfired. Mary was angered to find her plan of action for extortion through forcible occupation had an undesired result, since it had ushered in the very court case she had not wanted. She had acted unethically and unlawfully on Mr. Crack's bad advice.

Mary took refuge in wilful blindness. Mary's decision to extort a settlement payment through intimidation was undertaken on the advice of lawyer friend, Mr. Crack. She knew she had not behaved properly and was worried the Family Court judge will frown upon her refusal to vacate unless there was a private settlement outside the due process of Family Law. She decided to play dumb, that is to, legally speaking, deny *mens rea* or bad intent. If questioned she had been tutored to say she was a migrant, not aware of Australian law, and was acting innocently.

The lawyer was lawless. Incredibly, Mary's lawyer had advised illegality and more. Lawyer Mr Crack's advice defies understanding, as it meant the violation of the law fell within the bounds of his professional calling.   Mr. Crack, an Australian registered practitioner, was unbecomingly advising Mary to do nothing less than actually break the law on at least three fronts.

- For one thing, Mary's forced occupancy was illegal. There was no joint ownership of the family home. Shaun was its sole owner. That meant Mary resided in the home by reason of his permission to do so; she had no automatic legal right of occupation under the Family Law Act. Once Shaun's permission for Mary's occupation of the premises is withdrawn, she must leave. That is the law. Moreover, Shaun had offered her alternative accommodation, but she had refused his invitation to accompany him to his rented facility when he left the sold family home. Furthermore, she had been formally asked to vacate and offered an advance of $20K for other alternative rental accommodation on 28 December by Shaun's lawyer Gianna.

- Besides that illegality, another loomed large on the horizon: a future breach of contract. There was a legal sales contract on the property in place promising vacant possession to the buyer. So refusing to vacate would have involved a violation of contract terms involving a third party, namely the purchaser of the property.

- Making matters worse, there was in addition more than a whiff of blackmail. Mary's lawyer was advocating the odious criminal act of extorting by threat an informal private settlement outside the 'due process' procedures laid down in the Family Law Act. One interpretation is that the lawyer was advising a classic mafia-like shakedown of Shaun.

But playing with fire proved harmless. None of the above practices, despite being glaringly obvious, were at a threshold that attracted the official attention of the judge in the Family Court case at the Interim Hearing on 30 January. The judge's silence was deafening on Mary's extortion attempt that had brought on the court case and the expense of $15K imposed on Shaun by her action.

It was as if Mary had done nothing wrong. The home circumstances featuring the fear-inspiring forces of blackmail (a criminal offence), intimidation (a form of psychological violence, also criminal), and high financial cost, all unfairly imposed on an ailing old man, were recorded in court documents. But they attracted no public response from the judge in the Family Court proceedings. Mary was relieved she did not have to reimburse Shaun the court cost of $15K he incurred to force her to leave the apartment.

Shaun just had his first taste of unfairness from the legal system. These matters were outside the concern of the legal system; innocent victims had no hope of legal consideration, let alone legal compensation. Apparent blackmail and psychological intimidation were marked by legal impunity and carried the day. Mary got a free pass whilst Shaun lost $15K and suffered psychological violence. How could matters possibly get worse for Shaun?

But become worse they did – much worse.

3.2 The Plot Thickens

It was a hollow victory. Although Shaun won the case on 30 January, it was a victory that was pyrrhic to the core. The Family Court Order required Mary to vacate the home premises and gave Shaun "exclusive possession" by 3 February. Although the Family Court Order for Shaun was the logical upshot of a causal chain of events, Mary saw it as a calculated insult. So it is understandable that Mary would have an ace up her sleeve that made a mockery of the Family Court decision even as it was made. We shall later return to say much more on Mary's arrogant ploy that had been thoughtfully planned behind the scenes ahead of the Family Court hearing.

Before the Family Court proceedings commenced, an Alleluia moment for Mary had been a ghastly blow for Shaun. Shaun received a phone call from a police officer while waiting for his case to be called: there was a restraining order (that is, a protective order, technically referred to as Apprehended Violence Order or AVO) issued against him. He immediately asked what he had done to deserve it and was curtly told to come over and collect the document. A badly shaken Shaun reeled at the dire tidings from the blockbuster. He was standing beside his lawyer in the courthouse foyer at the time the news hit. His lawyer had to reassure him and find him a seat. Neither Shaun nor lawyer Gianna knew at the time that one of the specific provisions of the restraining order denied Shaun access to the sold premises for one year.

The situation transformed. The Family Court case, a civil matter, had now seamlessly degenerated into a Local Court case with a criminal dimension to it. Shaun faced the disgrace of a public trial where he was already declared guilty and would have to prove his innocence. Mary had pulled a gun during a fight with clubs, thereby altering the dynamics of the case. For Shaun, the mess metastasised.

That was a stroke of brilliance from the artful triumvirate. Mary could not help a slight smile of satisfaction during the Family Court proceedings; thanks to the conspiracy hatched with son Ian and lawyer Mr. Crack, the three birds of a feather had pulled a fast one on two courts of law. Mary had failed to disclose to the Family Court on 30 January that she had pre-emptively undermined the Family Court Order by filing a criminal complaint on 22 January denying Shaun access to the premises for one year on the ground that he had threatened her with violence at that address. Neither had she told the Local Court about the impending Family Court Order to eject her from that same address.

Consider this: Mary had done no less than play two courts of law against each other. She knew full well she had already *denied* Shaun access to the property by means of her police complaint on 22 January at the time that she agreed in writing to *allow* Shaun exclusive access to his property in the Family Court proceedings on 30 January. Mary was never one bit concerned that she had signed two conflicting legal documents that seemed to smack of snubs, if not contempt, of two courts of law. Mary had practiced to play possum if she were challenged about the transgressions. In spite of all the high-handed hanky-panky, Mary saw little reason to quake in her boots; sang-froid prevailed.

The Family Court Order was neutered. It had no effect because the restraining order (AVO) denying property access overrode the Family Court Order giving Shaun sole access. Consequently, Shaun's denial of access to the sold property continued despite the successful Family Court Order at high cost.

It was a strategic victory for Mary. But playing with fire proved harmless. None of her questionable behaviours were at a threshold that attracted the attention of the judge in the Family Court case at the Interim Hearing on 30 January. Mary, with help from her son and lawyer friend, had redefined the contours of the case and regained proactive control of the situation by adopting a set of alarmist tactics.

3.3 Ominous Lead-up

The situation was farcical. Shaun had to deal with conflicting orders from two courts of law acting independently of each other. Mary had withheld information from two judicial officers, causing them to make conflicting decisions due to being kept in the dark by Mary – suggestive of an element of trickery.

The mosaic of how such a ludicrous situation arose is now pieced together. This is important for gaining insight into the tandem behaviours of Mary and two courts of law – and its broader implications for social justice.

The past explains the present. After Mary's bombshell announcement of wanting to separate on 18 October, Shaun and Mary continued to share the same bed till he moved out on 24 December. Mary's extortionary demand for a settlement at 70 percent of the asset pool was made in early November following her inability stop the property sale that *she* had previously wanted. She had thereafter begun to spend most of the day in her son Ian's house, being picked up after breakfast, and being dropped off after dinner, to spend the night with Shaun. The couple spoke only when necessary.

Leaving home did not mean leaving off. Even after he had vacated the family home on 24 December, Shaun continued to visit his former family home to wash his clothes because he had no laundry facilities at his new place. He was still paying for all the utility services at his former family home while living away from it. Since he used to clean the home apartment at least twice a week, he carried on with the practice because Mary had a back problem; after all, the sold apartment needed to be handed over to the buyer in spick and span condition. At the back of his mind he feared Mary could change the locks and prevent him from going through with the sale of the property. On several occasions he brought Chinese take-away meals to share with Mary. She shared Christmas cake with him on the day after Christmas that she had got from her family, after having spent Christmas day with them.

The serving of Family Court papers was a turning point. All remaining cordiality went up in smoke on 10 January when court papers were served on Mary requiring her to attend a hearing on 30 January, at which appearance she was going to be ordered to vacate. Sensing she would be on the warpath, Shaun did not thereafter enter his apartment while she was there.

A new strategy was urgently required by Mary. Getting the court papers was a game-changer for Mary and eldest son Ian. That was because their strategy of attempting to privately extort 70/30 outside the due process of the legal system using the contract of sale as coercive leverage, had crumbled about their ears. They angrily panicked. Only somehow attaining the hallowed 70/30 settlement goal would nail it for them.

3.4 Raising the Stakes

A fusion of panic and fury fuelled Mary's motivation for revenge. The latest insult of being threatened with ejection had come on top of earlier humiliation. Being refused to be heard when she attempted to stop the sale of the property was enough egg on her face; now Mary faced the added affront to her dignity of being thrown out of her own home to which she had entitlement as a wife – or so she thought. Cultural considerations kicked in to feed her agitation at the poetic justice. What will people think? The shame of it! Besides, where was she to go? At son Ian's place she would need to dislodge one of the two adult grandchildren by occupying one of their rooms.

Other reasons contributed to Mary going ballistic. She had no appetite for a legal case, but had got one all the same. Mary's well laid plans had fallen flat. She never imagined she would fail so miserably in a strategy that after all had been craftily formulated by lawyer friend, Mr. Crack. Mary was also angered by the fact that information about her overseas income and assets had to be disclosed to Shaun for the first time in 20 years.

Shaun feared he had upset an applecart. He knew he had spoiled the well thought out strategic plan Mary and son Ian had been banking on to take the loot and run. He knew he had provoked them into lashing out, unleashing forces in a permissive arena that would spin wildly out of control due the absence of moral restraints on the duo. His fears were amply justified.

Mary reached meltdown. A tearfully livid Mary phoned around to smear Shaun by bluntly portraying him as a wife-beater, mistress-keeper, and financial-abuser. She had even made a vitriolic call for the first time ever to Shaun's ex-wife to convey to her the allegedly uncomplimentary things said about her by Shaun in court testimony – a breach of section 121 of the Family Law Act. As part of a campaign she told a mutual friend: "I'll make sure he ends up with nothing." To another she had said: "He never knew who I really am."

Mary was far from happy. To make matters worse, she was harassed by the process of getting legal aid, which she finally managed to get in time for the court hearing on 30 January. Legal aid is only given to those in need, but Mary was not in need because she had been offered an advance of $20K by Gianna, Shaun's lawyer, on 28 December. Mary qualified for legal aid by withholding information about that offer; she managed to fool the system by feigning poverty and successfully portraying herself as a maltreated wife in a desperate financial situation.

But that had knock-on effects. Mary had to substantiate the false image of penury-cum-victim she had projected to fraudulently claim legal aid. Such affirmation of credibility took the form of a police complaint, which was nevertheless justified on several other grounds as well. Subsequent events indicate the sham application for legal aid cramped her style, pushed her into extreme action, and hampered early settlement.

Mary had earlier sought the help of women's support facilities. She went to 'Mission Australia,' a Christian charity combating homelessness, in mid-December while she was still sharing her bed with Shaun. Mary told them she needed emergency housing because of the "unforeseen" sale of her house that threatened her with homelessness. She knew she had to twist the truth to strengthen her case. They told her she could be helped only if she has been abused. So she gave up on that option of seeking shelter and stuck to her guns of forcibly occupying the apartment until the demanded money materialized.

The serving of the court papers prompted Mary to go 'Mission Australia' once again. Recalling what the Program Manager had stated about abuse, she returned to the same organisation seeking a written certificate stating she had lived through years of domestic violence. That included her husband withholding medical treatment, physically assaulting her, and financially abusing her. She had not mentioned anything about the alleged maltreatment on her first visit a month earlier. That time she wanted accommodation, this time she wanted revenge. The certificate was readily issued for the asking by the Program Manager; no probing questions asked or evidence required.

Mary then went to the 'Domestic Violence Advocacy Group' offices. She was warmly welcomed and found the empathy comforting. Their magnanimity and case management support soothed her disappointment from her initial gambit of extortion being in tatters. The advice and information provided were generous. Their input into her testimony was eloquent and substantial. The kind people there were a tower of strength and were inspirational in strengthening her resolve to go the whole hog.

Mary was emboldened by her empowerment. A fortified Mary ramped up matters several notches by filing a police complaint. That dramatic escalation of the conflict was undertaken with the backing of her eldest son Ian, their present fury blinding them to its future complications.

3.5 No Trespassing

A police complaint was filed on the evening of 22 January. A fire-breathing Mary was in a 'no holds barred' mood when, accompanied by son Ian and his wife, she stalked into the local police station on that climactic evening. It was about a week after she had visited 'Mission Australia' and the 'Domestic Violence Advocacy Group' and a week before the scheduled Interim Hearing at the Family Court to eject her. She was goaded by blind rage that had been triggered by the court case having been brought against her wishes, as well as by the collateral insult from the threat of being ejected from her home.

While the overall aim of Mary's incendiary police complaint was to boost her monetary claim in the Family Court case, her immediate need was to deny Shaun entry to the property from which her expulsion was imminent.

Mary was at first uneasy, but soon settled down once she had her pre-prepared statement out of her handbag. With confidence from being armed with the 'Mission Australia' certificate, she read from a statement prepared with formidable input from her son Ian and the various women's welfare people she had consulted. Most of the statement was in the Australian vernacular, the idiom of which was alien to her, but which she felt suitably filled the bill. Reflecting her white-hot anger, the intemperate three-page police complaint alleged 20 years of regular physical assaults, one unleashed as recently as 18 October (about three months back), 12 years of supporting a mistress, and severe financial deprivation throughout the marriage.

Mere words did the trick, Mary was made to believe. From talking with people in the support organisations as well as her lawyer friend, Mary gained the impression that charges of violence brought in the criminal court would give her the upper hand vis-a-vis Shaun. She was under the impression that would be so even though they lacked a shred of corroborative evidence and were inconsistent with wider contextual and situational facts. The possibility of cross-examination never crossed her mind. Mary could not see why the absence of evidence should deter her when just words had, up to then, unfailingly served her purpose – that is, made mud stick with a vengeance. She noted with satisfaction that serious enough assertions, when expressed with vehemence, automatically induced the wheels of justice to turn decidedly in her favour, and to the detriment of Shaun.

Several advantages accrued by bringing even unprovable charges. From discussion with her advisers Mary believed they would: automatically give her the coercive advantage (restraining orders are issued without inquiry, so Shaun immediately gets put on the back foot); intimidate Shaun (cause him weakness from stress and lower his resolve); cast defamatory aspersions (destroy Shaun's self image of a scholar and professional); and bolster her claims under the Family Law (which is well designed to seamlessly accommodate such allegations).

Mary expected Shaun's resolve to crumble. Her women's welfare advisers had assured her that, after such indefensible abuse of her as alleged, Shaun would be arrested. He would then simply give in and accept the restraining order against him on a permanent basis. After all, that is what usually happened in the domestic violence cases they were accustomed to dealing with, typically involving aggressive dregs of humanity.

Mary's credibility rested on withheld information. Specifically, in stating her case to the police on 22 January, Mary failed to disclose facts that would cast doubt upon her uncorroborated allegations. Hidden from the police was contrary information of a direct, circumstantial, and other exculpatory nature – the sort that would call her accusations into question in cross-examination.

Featuring in Mary's police statement were the following. She stated that her family knew nothing about 20 years of assaults till 18 October of that year, but did not disclose they lived nearby and had frequent and close interaction over the two decades. She explained she did not come in immediately after the last alleged assault on 18 October because she was due to have a colonoscopy on 28 November. Besides her silence on the need for a time lapse of over five weeks, she did not mention that it was Shaun who took her to the hospital for her colonoscopy on 28 November and stayed with her for the several hours it took. She also failed to explain the near two-month delay between then and the timing of the current complaint, or mention the 'ejection papers' received in the interim. She was silent about all that prolonged overseas travel with Shaun over 20 years, the last one for three months, completed just a month before the separation in October. Nothing was said about being dropped off at her home by her family every evening to share Shaun's bed – and that for two months after revealing to them Shaun's alleged violent character. Neither did she mention that the apartment she was seeking to debar Shaun from was solely owned by Shaun, that it had been sold because of her demands, and that she was in illegal occupation. And she certainly did not mention the looming Family Court action that was to going to force her to vacate her current accommodation so Shaun could have "exclusive possession."

The police-initiated Local Court action was swift. The matter was time-sensitive; Mary was to be urgently protected. None of the foregoing factors was taken into account in the prompt issuance of the restraining order against Shaun that, among other things, denied him access to the sold property. The long arm of the law was too short for the purpose of verifying the truthfulness of complaints. Immediate automatic action had to be taken by the Local Court to protect Mary from further violence, time being of the essence.

Mary's plans had proceeded like clockwork. She was pleased her changed tack was swinging things her way once again. She expected Shaun to be arrested and remanded following her police statement on 22 January, as told to her would happen. That would teach him a lesson he would find hard to forget. To top it off, she had sabotaged Shaun's case in the Family Court whereby he was seeking access to the sold property. That she did by thwarting the forthcoming Family Court Order expected to give Shaun exclusive access to that property.

Such is the backdrop to the Local Court's restraining order that overrode the Family Court Order giving Shaun sole access to the sold premises after 3 February. Shaun was back to square one, while Mary believed she had succeeded in subverting the property sale.

3.6 Victimized Victim

Shaun was in a fix following the Family Court Interim Hearing. How to overcome the daunting predicament caused by conflicting court orders? Answer: engage a barrister.

Frenzied legal action was taken. After the court case on 30 January, Shaun needed to hurriedly file an emergency motion in the Local Court and have his barrister see the magistrate in Chambers to have the provision in the Local Court Order, denying Shaun access to his property, removed. Only then he could proceed to act on the Family Court Order giving him "exclusive possession." There are no prizes for guessing that there were legal costs associated with the Local Court's removal of the restriction on the Family Court Order that were additional to those already incurred for the latter.

The legal action in the Local Court was surprisingly smooth sailing. When notified about the conflict between the court orders, the magistrate did not say a word about the blatant skulduggery that had occasioned his intervention. Nor had he expressed concern about the unilateral punishments imposed on Shaun in the form of anxiety and financial cost. The magistrate made a virtue out of necessity when he simply removed the Local Court restriction on Shaun's access to his property without demurring. It was just a routine matter for the magistrate, but only because nothing happened about Mary's mischief in causing conflict between the Court Orders and the associated extra pecuniary costs for Shaun. No sweat. No commiseration either.

Shaun was made to pay for Mary's wrongs. The fallout to Shaun was in the form of monetary and psychological costs.

Mary's actions were beyond the pale. Shaun had to get the Family Court Order to stop Mary doing what she should never have done in the first place, namely refuse to vacate the property she had wanted sold. Then having got the Family Court Order, he had to act again to get a Local Court Order to enable him to act on the Family Court Order. Once again something happened that should never have happened. The total financial cost to Shaun of Mary's actions was $17K. Since that was not of concern to the Family Court at any stage, the money was never recovered or compensated for.

The mental cost borne was attributable to psychological violence. The torment, in the form of threat and intimidation, impaired Shaun's ability to sleep and eat. There was high anxiety for a lonely old man of 76 years of age with a heart condition. To Shaun, the Local Court case was more an inconvenience and put-down than a threat since he knew he was innocent. For this reason it paled in relation to Mary's extortionist demand that used the sales contract as leverage. Shaun experienced constant anguish fearing a breach of the sales contract. Additionally, preventing Shaun from acting on the Family Court Order, by bringing the countermanding restraining order, worsened his deteriorating mental health. That drove him to seek medical help.

3.7 Between the Cracks

Mary vacated the sold apartment on the Family Court ordered date. She did so in a state of rage, vowing more retaliation. She was humiliated and inconvenienced. Being forced to leave was shameful. And due to time pressure she had to settle for second rate free lance removalists to move the household furniture into storage. Even though she had been given an advance of $35K from the asset pool, she opted to move into eldest son Ian's place rather than into rental accommodation.

There was a lot to move. She took away the majority of the quality furniture, including leather lounge suites and massive TV, as well as all of the several dinner services and crystal ware. While she was sad to leave the beautiful family home, she was comforted by the knowledge there were better things to come.

The property sale concluded. After being notified of Mary's departure by his lawyer, Shaun was able enter the premises to clean the apartment and successfully pass the inspection for handing the property over on the scheduled date of 6 February. Then money changed hands.

But the sale proceeds never reached Shaun; they were sequestered. Shaun's hopefulness, namely that the stash of cash from the property sale would enable him to finally get his hands on his life's savings as a war chest for fighting the legal battle ahead, turned out to be tragically forlorn – a pipe dream. Mary's lawyer required that the funds be blocked until the case was concluded. Shaun protested, but lawyer Gianna said he had no choice. That was a horrific paradox, as Shaun was being denied money needed to protect that money. So on top of everything else, Shaun was slap bang in the midst of a personal financial crisis as never before.

The case was not concluded for a further 13 months. In the meantime, Shaun was forced to use his impeccable credit rating to get himself a personal loan of $20K to meet legal and other expenses. Over that period, while Mary was on legal aid, Shaun lived on loans, from hand-to-mouth, alone in his cold studio apartment, bracing for the next legal invoice. Shaun found himself incarcerated in the prison of debt, with every day of court delay being a far-from pleasant experience.

Compared to Shaun's plight, Mary was sitting pretty. She had received legal aid and also an advance settlement of $35K while living in her son Ian's home, and later in a retirement hostel, on her full pension. She never felt richer; there was enough income for both her and son Ashley. She had nothing to lose and everything to gain. The similar sum of $35K received by Shaun was immediately gobbled up by costs for lawyers and the two wasteful court orders. One was the Family Court Order to force Mary to vacate and the other was the Local Court Order to enable Shaun to act on the Family Court Order.

We pause to take stock of what happened here. We do so without in any way questioning the truthfulness or otherwise of Mary's dreadful allegations against Shaun to the police. Judging the veracity of Mary's allegations against Shaun will have to await the outcome in the Local Court case, reported later *con mucho colorido* – that is, in colourful terms.

The permissiveness from treacherous gaps in the legal system is hard to miss. We concisely recapitulate, the walk back in time zeroing-in on the several pitfalls in the legal processes to this stage, so here goes: Mary had wanted the property sold so she could go off on her own; but when she realised she might not get as much money as she wanted, she attempted to stop the sale to carry on as before; when she could not do so, she refused to vacate even though she had no legal right to remain in the family home once Shaun had left; she went outside the legal system to demand an unfair private settlement; Shaun had to incur unwarranted costs to make her vacate; but Mary did not have to pay any legal penalty for her extortionary threat, not even legal costs, because two judges let it ride; the successful court order to compel ejection was forestalled by Mary with a countermeasure imposed by the Local Court without any investigation; then Shaun had to take further legal action to be able to act on the Family Court Order; being able to act on the Family Court Order enabled him to conclude the house transaction, but not recover the court costs incurred or obtain the sale proceeds of his apartment; his offer of immediate settlement at 50/50 percent was summarily rejected delaying the end of the case; he needed to take out a loan to make ends meet in a condition of hardship for him that was absent for Mary.

Playing the angles had paid off for Mary. One thing highlighted in the unfolding story to this point is that Mary was able to adroitly game the system with the help of well-meaning and cosy contacts, including professionally dubious lawyers. She successfully pulled off daring stunts in the form of extortion and the signing of conflicting undertakings to different courts of law. In fact, there was impunity for a slew of process abuses, with the transgressions delivering, not punishment, but benefits in terms of revenge and money.

3.8 Institutional Failings

Although the legal system did deliver in the end, the process was rough; its qualities were hardly the touchstones of fairness. Navigating the judicial system was far more unfair for Shaun than it was for Mary. For Shaun, the worrisome reality of process laxity in a judicial system he thought he could rely upon for fairness, brought nothing but trouble and gave him much to worry about besides death. Mary's strategy, proactively undertaken with measured irony within an accommodating judicial system, is emblematic of institutional failure. That means official procedural laxity rears its unseemly head as a sign of the times.

The implication for society is worrisome. There is an unpleasant and perplexing compatibility between abuse of judicial processes and judicial disregard for it. Permissiveness from judicial tolerance enabled Mary's misconduct to fall between cracks in the judicial processes of two courts of law. No matter how you slice it, the conclusion is inescapable that process failures in judicial channels gave rise to repeated inaction or misaction at every turn, with the need for administrative pragmatism apparently outweighing the need for social fairness. Principles of fairness were conspicuous by their absence because an official blind eye was turned when a quizzically beady eye would have been just the thing. That justice can be delivered by dysfunctional judicial processes is already shown to be a contradiction in terms.

But now is not the end of the road for the tormenting tale on institutional unfairness. There is a long way yet to travel on a perilous road punctuated by twists and turns, humps and dips, potholes and quicksand. Disputants are condemned to persevere along a road lacking reliable institutional guardrails against unfairness, soldiering on towards a distant justice that would, in the end, be a road to riches for some and a road to ruin for others.

***

Chapter 4

RAGS TO RICHES: HERE COMES THE MONEY

4.1 Prime Culprit

Things were so different at the start. Twenty years before the separation Mary was thrilled Shaun was to give her a future in Australia. She told a friend whom she had bumped into at the airport when enplaning for Australia that for her lots of Christmases had come at once. The move to Australia gave Mary, at that time a low-income widow paying off a mortgage, the added advantage of being able to join six members of her immediate family then residing in Sydney. The youngest of her offspring, son Ashley, was able to get permanent residence at the same time as his mother on account of then being aged 17. All legal and application costs associated with the migration process for mother and son were met by recent husband, Shaun.

This son, Ashley, was the villain of the piece. He was behind the disastrous fate that befell the marriage and led to the devastation of two innocent lives. He was unable to get proper vocational qualifications or hold down a job. He had a nasty temper and had verbally abused his stepfather Shaun while living in his parent's apartment free of rent and board for over eight months. When Shaun complained to Mary that he had been abused in his own home during her stint in hospital, she had said: "If he goes, I go."

Ashley stayed. Shaun confined himself to his room out of embarrassment, as he had never before been spoken to with such disrespect. Due to cognitive dissonance, Shaun did not blame Mary for his humiliating circumstances, ascribing them to mother's love. But Mary's eldest son Ian, who was in frequent touch with her, knew something that Shaun was not conscious of: he told his mother, because the Family Law gave her the whip hand, she should stand firm and have Ashley stay put. That explains Mary's intimidating warning to Shaun about leaving him if Ashley had to go – arguably, a 'no-fault' backed threat that smacks of blackmail.

Let us pause to ponder the deeper meaning. The statistics reveal some half of all marriages end in separation. But that numerical piece of information understates the number of people trapped in ongoing family relationships that are unhappy because their rights are violated due to 'no-fault' empowerment. Shaun was oblivious to the obvious: his fundamental right to the peaceful enjoyment of his own home was denied, thanks to the intrusively overhanging threat of the 'no-fault' provision of the Family Law Act.

It was the case of an overstayed welcome. Ashley had never asked his stepfather if he may stay there or thanked him for the hospitality, perhaps out of a sense of culturally-driven entitlement. He considered it his prerogative to stay on for eight months, well beyond the three weeks his mother had initially said he would be there for. To Shaun's discomfort, he stayed on even after his parents had departed on overseas holidays, and was to use the place as a venue for meeting up with dubious girl friends.

4.2 Pennies from Heaven

The marriage opened financial doors. Under section 79(4) of the Family Law Act contributions to the marriage are of vital relevance in final settlement. So it is significant that because of her new-found support from Shaun, Mary's assets were secretly transferred to the adult offspring of her previous marriage. There was widow's cruse when the pecuniary efflux took the form of both capital and income.

Capital went. The proceeds from the sale of Mary's house and property were transferred to Mary's children without the knowledge and consent of Shaun. That was done despite her fully dependant status. Shaun found out about this transfer only later and ensured that it be officially recorded with the welfare agency Centrelink at the time he helped Mary to apply for a public pension.

Income also went. Hidden pensions flowed to secret places. Mary withheld information on her two overseas pensions from Shaun for the full duration of their marriage. She was angered when she was required to disclose this information for the divorce case, but only after things had turned grubby. One of the overseas pensions was from her employment in the foreign country, and the other a widow's pension.

The widow's pension was illegal. Receiving the widow's pension was prohibited by law once Mary re-married. She ensured its improper continuance by not changing her former married surname (not her maiden name) upon marriage to Shaun – most unusual for someone culturally shackled – and withholding information on her changed civil status from the foreign pensions authority.

Unbeknownst to Shaun, both foreign pensions were covertly given to her youngest son Ashley for 20 years. But the boldly withheld foreign pensions were the lesser non-contribution.

Even more brazen was the stealthy diversion to Ashley of the larger Australian pension. That happened right under Shaun's nose. When after ten years of residence in Australia Mary qualified for the age pension from the welfare agency Centrelink, Shaun helped in the application thinking it would contribute towards the household retirement income.

But Shaun's expectation was fanciful. Mary did not see her Centrelink pension money as contributing to the household with Shaun; she saw the money coming in her name as an assured solution to her son Ashley's chronic unemployment problem. What is more, when she realised that it was only a part pension because of Shaun's superannuation and assets, she felt she had been robbed by circumstances for which Shaun was responsible. Shaun owed her the forgone part of her pension. Consequently, Mary felt perfectly at ease in taking extra money from Shaun under the false pretence that it was for household expenses when in fact it was for the funding of her son Ashley's extravagant lifestyle that matched her own.

Ashley's financial wants, not needs, explain the marital crisis. We can confidently finger Mary's passion to secretly finance son Ashley's lavish lifestyle from the household budget as the primary cause of the marriage breakdown. A large portion of household cash, secretly siphoned off to Ashley from the outset of the marriage and for 19 years, is the crux of the matter.

Secretly given easy money funded conspicuous consumption for high living. Unemployed Ashley enjoyed a lifestyle that surpassed that of his three employed siblings almost beyond imagination. Covert funding financed Ashley's numerous overseas trips including to Asia and Europe, five-star hotel stays, and ongoing mortgage payments on Ashley's house property purchased with his mother's house sale proceeds. At the time of Ashley's second marriage at age 34, his only regular income was his mother's household monies, comprising her three pensions and saved grocery money, which manna had been assuredly falling his way for many years before then. Shaun had ignorantly paid tax on money his household never received.

Mary's monetary contribution to the marriage was a cavernous negative. The totality of three pensions, household grocery money, and capital funds transferred from Shaun's household to Ashley over the period of the marriage was estimated to exceed $304K in 2019 values. From a Family Law standpoint, that qualifies as non-contribution to the marriage. Astonishingly, it counted for nothing in the final 'no-fault' Family Court settlement, as explained in Chapter 10.

4.3 Cultural Clash

Mary was caught up in a clash of cultures. She was culturally driven to help her failed son. As she hailed from an Asian collectivistic culture, there was belief in a sort of family socialism when it came to money. That meant there needed to be sharing among members of the extended family; one should not ignore those other tribal members who are disadvantaged. Mary's culture-driven handout of household money to members of her tribe was, in the words of Francis Bacon (1561-1626), "the idol of the tribe" (a deep-rooted false notion).

That contrasts with the Western cultural value of individualism. Based on the Judeo-Christian ethic, it recognises the autonomy of the individual human being in society. It simplistic terms it means 'each one for oneself,' and comes with pride in being self-made and self-reliant. That embodies the notion of an honest penny and shuns "the bread of idleness".

Blood ties outweighed marriage vows. Shaun would not understand Asian cultural compulsions and so was better off not knowing about the money that had been unflinchingly siphoned from the household budget for many years. Mary had no qualms about stealthy money flows to Ashley, and Ashley had no compunction about secretly living off his mother as a grown man, even after marriage. He was hooked on the flow of easy money that had given him worldly ease for many years. Mother and son's actions found justification in the alien collectivistic cultural rationale that justified blood ties superseding loyalty to husband.

The husband's unstinting support of wife Mary meant unwitting enrichment of stepson Ashley – and the expedited shrinking of Shaun's asset pool. The surreptitious money flow from mother to son had been possible only because all Mary's expenses were met by her husband. That included her health insurance premiums and other expenses for medicines, medical services, cosmetics, telephones, rent, overseas trips, domestic travel, and routine living. It was handy that Mary had a secondary platinum credit card with a $20K limit.

But hold on; let us not rush to judgement and condemn Mary. What was sickening parasitism for Shaun was culturally virtuous for Mary. Mary had a mindset that, although may appear deplorable from a Western point of view, made sense from an Asian standpoint. Her support for her failed son qualified as virtuous righteousness in terms of the Asian cultural value of collectivism. That culture-coloured view was the expressly stated rationalisation by the wife of Mary's eldest son Ian of the stealthy money transfers to brother-in-law Ashley, in which she was complicit.

That said, it must be acknowledged that virtue does not mean 'anything goes.' There is nothing absolute about moral righteousness in virtuous conduct as one person's act of religious virtue can be another person's barbaric bomb blast. According to philosopher Albert Camus (1913-60), "Virtue cannot separate itself from reality without becoming a principle of evil." The implication is that, what is good and bad must be decided in relevant context, namely in terms of Australian values and official expectations. Otherwise, in the words of Bernard Mandeville in *Fable of the Bees* (1705), "virtue was hypocrisy." Hence, in the described Australian context and family circumstances, the income-sharing idol was arguably a false god unworthy of worship by Mary. If the above philosophers are to be believed, a culture-bound virtuous position can then also be a refuge for scoundrels.

Culture indoctrinates. Minds that are brainwashed by alien cultural values can be blind to the true purpose of Centrelink age pensions paid for by Australian taxpayers. Mary's culturally narrow perceptual lens revealed the Centrelink money as her money that she had a right to spend in any way she pleased. It mattered not to her that the pension was being paid to her because it was Shaun who had enabled her to get immigration status by marrying her, and had thereafter supported her with his earned income for ten years till she qualified.

Mary rationalised dishonesty. She refused to face up to the reality that the unearned money falling in her lap was officially intended for self-support within the Australian household, and as compensating retired Shaun's household for past support and tax paid on her behalf. She did not care that Shaun was paying tax on money she was withholding from him. Mary had no pangs of conscience about secretly gifting the entire sum and more for high end living to third parties in violation of the expectations of her husband and government officialdom. Her raison d'être enabled her to live happily with her clueless husband for many years. Ignorance was indeed bliss.

But "Where ignorance is bliss, 'tis folly to be wise" (Thomas Gray, 1742). Shaun's wising up to Mary's systematic secret appropriation of his household funds for some 19 years caused him emotional distress, if only because he thought there was a betrayal of confidence. The money had been taken under false pretences; the deception meant that cheating was going on behind his back, even as Mary shared her life with him. For Shaun, it was beyond belief she could abuse trust like that.

But Shaun did not jump in to suddenly confront Mary on such a fundamental matter. While he hated conflict, it also subconsciously dawned on him that he had been living in fool's paradise; his marriage was a flimsy house of cards. However, he was reluctant to act – allowing the menacing truth to lie dormant due to cognitive dissonance. Shaun sullenly watched the situation quietly for several more months till Mary was completely recovered from her illness when, about a year later, he gathered the courage to finally take the bull by the horns.

4.4 Riding High

Shaun's household expenditure featured a dual outflow. One outlay was above board and the other underhand. Mary's clandestine pensions-cum-grocery household money transfers to son Ashley took place over the same period as husband Shaun was spending over $62K on medical payments for wife Mary, as well as a further $400K on her leisure travel (in 2019 values) from a fixed asset pool. Much of this was evidenced by medical receipts, credit card transactions, and passport information, as was officially documented in discovery (reported in Chapter 7). Together the couple jointly undertook some 132 overseas trips over 20 years to all parts of the globe including to the UK, USA, Canada, Europe, China, Thailand, and the Caribbean, plus several cruises and countless road and rail tours. All this was besides the money spent on maintaining a generally high level of everyday living.

Generosity trumped suspicion due to cognitive dissonance, as previously explained. Despite Shaun's hunch about what was happening to household grocery money, he did not hold back on his support for Mary. Important to what comes later is the fact that Shaun spent $5800 to purchase a high-end hairpiece made of matching human hair for Mary just one year prior to the separation. Mary had lost her hair due to chemotherapy and had taken to wearing a scarf. The purchase of the wig was made without any request from his wife. It was a pleasant surprise for Mary. Shaun took her to a hairdresser friend who used past photographs to copy Mary's previous hairstyle. Thereafter Mary no longer felt she needed to be house-bound. There was resumption of prolonged overseas travel over several months. This information on Shaun's gifting of the wig out of love and caring is important, because Mary later used it to disparage Shaun and nullify its benefit to her.

The Family Court did not seem to consider the foregoing information to be of any relevance in the final settlement. Nonetheless, the secret transfers from mother to son are vital for the purpose of understanding and assessing the fairness of the final settlement outcome of the case reported in Chapter 9.

4.5 Creeping Suspicions

Faith dwindled. After over 19 years of trusting his wife with the household finances, Shaun stumbled on three pointers that raised suspicion most of the money supposedly taken for groceries and basic household expenses was not in fact being used for its claimed purpose.

Suddenly matters could no longer be taken for granted. There was shocking realisation that the fortnightly amount for groceries was oddly excessive. In 2019 values, Mary had $810 a fortnight available to spend on just groceries and sundry household goods. Shaun was astonished when recent Internet research had revealed a two-person household spent an average of only $290 a fortnight for the purpose. That would have been about right for Mary because, although the couple ate out often at Shaun's expense, they also often entertained the extended family to meals. Nothing was saved by Mary; every dollar had been inevitably spent at an equivalent inflation-adjusted level every fortnight when not travelling, and this practice had existed since the start of the relationship.

Further, there was a perplexing coincidence. Mary's suspiciously excessive outlay on groceries took place in a situation where son Ashley had an obviously extravagant lifestyle despite his unemployed status. In fact, he whooped it up in the fast lane and put his three employed siblings' plodding lifestyle well in the shade. Mary's over-egging of Ashley's pudding raised questioning eyebrows within the family and baffled Shaun who was at pains to reconcile Ashley's high living with his jobless status. A niggling suspicion was to gradually grow into great concern as to what might actually be happening to what Shaun considered was household grocery money.

Furthermore, Shaun personally made a disconcerting discovery. Shaun found grocery expenses by Mary were disturbingly excessive when he undertook routine grocery shopping for the first time, 18 years into the relationship. That was when Mary was under hospital and home treatment for anal cancer. Over this stressful period of about three months, Shaun took care of Mary 24/7, including almost daily trips for radiotherapy and other treatment, assisting with bathing, and doing whatever it took. Mary's family pitched in with meals and visited on an almost daily basis since they lived in nearby suburbs. Restaurant take-aways were frequently purchased because Shaun was unable to cook.

For the first time ever, Mary felt worried. There was distinct unease the new shopping arrangement would reveal what she had successfully hidden for many years. But she could do nothing about it. Her fears were justified when Shaun's undertaking of the grocery and take-away shopping cost much less than a third of what Mary had unwaveringly claimed for the purpose for 19 years. It confirmed his fears that trust in his wife had caused him to be asleep at the wheel and ignore numerous flashing warning signs over the years – a behaviour explained by cognitive dissonance. The realization he had been deceived for years finally struck home and sickened him with sadness.

At first Shaun, being cautious, tried the softly-softly approach. Several months after Mary had recovered from her illness, Shaun expressed to her some doubts about what was happening to household money. Mary promptly informed her eldest son Ian about the suspicions being expressed by Shaun. Mary was anticipating the query and was confident she could bluff him into believing her as he always took her at her word. She vehemently assured Shaun that all the money was indeed being spent on groceries and sundry household expenses.

Shaun was gaslighted – a classic sociopathic tactic. As psychologists would say, he was manipulated into self-doubt – that is, manoeuvred into questioning his own belief about what he knew was happening to household money. He had been prepared to let bygones be bygones if Mary had admitted the truth. But now he was confused, given that he had all along been hoping against hope he was mistaken about Mary's fishy money management practices. He opted to carry on as usual and silently further monitor the situation – that cognitive dissonance factor coming into play once again, this time with a vengeance.

However, life was not quite the same thereafter. While watching expenses, life went on as usual on the surface, including overseas travel. But there was a new growing underlying unease about what was really happening to lots of household retirement income. Mary was vaguely conscious of being watched but did not change her spending pattern. Shaun's feeling of mistrust caused a subtle despondency to pervade the relationship.

4.6 Watershed Development

Matters finally came to a head. A blow up took place on 26 February, about a year after suspicions first arose about household money being taken under false pretences. On that fateful day Shaun accused Mary of hoodwinking him. The remonstration by Shaun was to the effect that the deceitful transfer of household monies was unacceptable and had to cease. The superannuation savings were run down after extensive travel up to then and the recent heavy unexpected medical expenses for cancer treatment; son Ashley was married, had his own household, and should take care of himself; in any case, a cutback on expenditures was necessary because of unknown future medical expenses from possible recurrence of Mary's cancer and Shaun's ongoing heart condition subsequent to bypass surgery. If Ashley was in real need of help, the money had to be given openly from the both of them.

Mary was silent during Shaun's unusual outburst. She accepted there was righteous indignation behind the confrontation, and was in any case conscious of her upper hand under the Family Law. She decided she needed to consult son Ian on what to do. The routine of life resumed.

After a few days, and after having consulted eldest son Ian, Mary informed Shaun she would cease the support payments to son Ashley. Shaun assured her he was there to help Ashley should the need arise. But Mary knew what Shaun did not; it was not the end of the matter and that her bombshell standby plan would need to be activated. But not just yet though, as they were shortly due to head off to Asia and Europe for four months.

The irreconcilable difference proved a watershed in the relationship. Subsequent events were to show that stopping Mary's secret funding of her married son's lavish lifestyle was a turning point that doomed the relationship, although Shaun was blind to the writing on the wall at the time. It was an unbridgeable chasm since what Mary saw as righteous support for Ashley was repugnant thievery for Shaun. Its discovery spelled the beginning of the end and culminated in Mary's bombshell announcement of wanting to separate seven months later, on 18 October.

4.7 Noxious Combination

Pondering on the preceding information brings to light the home truth that Mary's alien cultural trait was also abnormal. That is, Mary's behaviour, culturally different, was in addition socially deviant. Cultural compulsions would not by themselves provide enough of an irresistible impulse for Mary's highly questionable practices. The exhibited behaviour clearly goes against usual human social norms and mores, regardless of culture. They can probably also be attributed to the personality disorder of Sociopathy, as suggested by two psychologists close to the case and referred to in sections 7.3 and 9.3 – the confluence of the sociological with the psychological shedding greater explanatory light on Mary's conduct.

The key general trait of a sociopath is a lack of conscience and a specific manifestation is marrying for money. That is according to expert Martha Stout in her book *The Sociopath Next Door: The Ruthless Versus the Rest of Us* (2005). Sociopaths lack guilt, remorse, and are expert pathological liars. Besides the systematic secret money transfers to her offspring, other unconscionable practices were demonstrated by Mary with a good deal of regularity.

The more flagrant in a pattern of anti-social behaviour were: falsehoods to her family about Shaun; supporting her son's verbal assault on Shaun within the family residence; untruths about her income and assets; withholding critical information in sworn statements to two courts of law; the signing of a false agreement to permit access to the sold property; fraudulently obtaining legal aid; false claims to women's support agencies; fraudulently drawing the foreign widow's pension; forcibly occupying the sold apartment; extortionary demand outside the due process of Family Law; slanderous phone calls for a blatant smear job on Shaun; a greedy settlement demand; violating section 121 of the Family Law Act; gaslighting; cooking up court testimony and denying obviously generous benefits from Shaun (in Chapter 5); suppressing information in discovery (in section 7.4); and threatening her mentally disabled stepson with homelessness (in section 9.1). It appears this raft of mischievous behaviours combine to constitute quite a pathological package embodying desensitised morality.

Appearances can be deceiving. Sociopaths are known to be charming social predators who abuse their partners. It is in the nature of sociopaths to play a part on the surface and to exploit favourable situations while leading a hidden double life. Chillingly, sociopaths are unconscious of their flaws as social human beings, seeing the world through the prism of self-interest. For them, feelings are facts – implying delusiveness. Sociopathy, together with related narcissism and psychopathy, are toxic anti-social personality disorders affecting up to 25 percent of the population (Stout 2005). In technical parlance, Mary's behaviour displayed a pathologically impaired cognitive function.

4.8 Grave Conclusions

The preceding information raises issues requiring serious thought. Implicit in the situation is that Shaun faced Hobson's choice: either he keeps silent about the violation of his rights and his knowing about the secret money transfers and carries on with the relationship, or he puts a stop to them only to face separation. (Take your pick.) A toxic mix from Mary's alien cultural values being compounded with Sociopathy, had Shaun trapped from day one; he was inescapably damned if he did and damned if he didn't. Finally, after 20 years, his overindulged chickens came home to roost.

Mother and son were hand in glove, Mary and eldest son Ian had known of Shaun's predicament all along. Shaun was unconscious about it, being blinded by love and trust of his wife. Although Mary always knew she had the upper hand, she also knew she was skating on thin ice. Mother and son were ready with a Plan B should Shaun get too far out of line or the secret money transfers to Ashley come to light. They had checked out their position with lawyer Mr. Crack and were comforted they had the friendly 'no-fault' Family Law on their side. The success of Plan B depended on it. Mary was to later tell a friend that Shaun, despite his education, was a fool who never realised that she and son Ian had him at their mercy for all those years.

The evidence shows up the 'no-fault' Family Law's capability as a ubiquitous spook. The information in this chapter adds to that in Chapter 2 to reveal it as a universal regime that reaches into all family homes at all times – implying ever-present public intrusion into private space for good or ill. Its permanent presence means it can at any time influence everyday behaviours in the several ways demonstrated in this tale. The evidence shows it gave Mary and son Ian the green light and necessary cover to play dirty in different ways. Specifically, the 'no-fault' Family Law empowered Mary and son Ian for behaviours featuring blackmail, intimidation, and exploitation. When a personality disorder like Sociopathy is present, the 'no-fault' Family Law jointly with readily available restraining orders (see section 3.5), can ominously hover over relevant family relationships like an omnipresent sword of Damocles.

There is obvious evidence of what psychologists call 'hypergamy' in the marriage. That refers to the usual – and socially acceptable – practice of marrying to elevate one's status. Shaun was a high-value target. But here that marry-up practice appears to have been accompanied by what looks a lot like the hallmarks of a mercenary syndrome. That refers to motivation driven by the desire for material gain, in this case the love of money outweighing the love of Shaun.

The combination is noxious. The mercenary syndrome by itself does not necessarily involve dishonesty. However, when driven by Sociopathy, it can include forays into the arena of deviousness, as did indeed happen in this case. Then the mix of hypergamy and Sociopathy makes what is culturally acceptable degenerate to the socially despicable.

It appears the Sociopathy-driven marry-for-money strategy in this tale of 'From Rags to Riches' was enabled and encouraged by the 'no-fault' provision of the Family Law Act. Improper practices, however brazen, appear to seamlessly dovetail into that accommodating provision. 'No-fault' removes boundaries that would otherwise have inhibited partners lacking moral restraints due to anti-social personality disorders from cheekily abusing the legal system.

As lines in the sand stand erased, the resultant ethical void emboldens a sense of entitlement, encouraging the afflicted to take as much ground as they can get. That means, Mary's behaviour is not just about her, but also about 'no-fault' that puts the wind at the back of her apparent anti-social pathology. Other examples of dubious behaviour reported throughout this book repeatedly illustrate the existence of such an insidious side-effect of the Family Law Act. That suggests the Family Law as implemented is weak in coping with personality disorder-caused abnormality in human behaviour. It therefore qualifies as a deficiency to be corrected when the judicial reforms are presented.

***

Chapter 5
SCATHING RESPONSE: DEFENCE BY ATTACK

5.1 Prelude to Perjury

Hello? Has anyone heard of something called perjury? In case you don't know, that means: knowingly and wilfully making a false statement about a material fact.

It was a case of killing two birds with one stone. Mary's allegations against Shaun were the subject of criminal complaint in the Local Court. They were mostly the same as what her Family Court testimony was going to be – essentially, one testimony in two courts. So the validity of her mostly singular allegations was going to be tested in open Local Court proceedings before later being considered by the Family Court. The idea was that success in alleging maltreatment in the Local Court would bolster Mary's case for settlement in the Family Court. Mary had been made to understand by the social networks she leaned on that the Local Court case would never be contested by Shaun; the case was just a formality – a certain 'walk over' for Mary.

Lawyers are required to ensure truth in client testimony. This is especially so when such statements are drawn up in response to information from the opposition that is already on the table. Professional propriety demands that they ensure assertions made by their client are backed up with evidence as far as possible, are not exaggerated or internally inconsistent, and have a general tenor of persuasive plausibility. That was the yardstick applied by Shaun's lawyer Gianna, who was keen to make sure Shaun's testimony was a declaration of truth.

But Mary's legal aid lawyer used disparaging testimony for effect, namely to soften the opposition. Truth was not something of interest to him; he was prepared to readily sign off on barefaced lies, as will soon be apparent. The lawyer was aware that attacking testimony would hurt the opposition but not be challenged even though lacking believability. That haughty presumption can probably be attributed to easygoing processes in the 'no-fault' Family Court and readily available restraining orders, as earlier described in section 3.5.

Anticipated impunity was a green light for perjury. When Mary gained the impression there were no unpleasant consequences for false testimony to the Family Court, she and eldest son Ian went to town with damaging allegations contrived with gay abandon, in consultation with women's support groups. Therefore, rather than being a guiding hand, Mary's legal aid lawyer was happy to be a conduit for her vendetta. It is small wonder that he had no interest in giving objective advice to Mary about the harmful complications from her wanting to target a disabled boy's property. Because subsequent developments are shown to expose Mary's court allegations as reeking of perjury, it can be confidently pronounced that integrity was not among her lawyer's strong points.

We uncover here the unedifying phenomenon of sharp practice in vogue. As Hollywood is to movies, the lawyer's office was to fabrications. It was becoming increasingly clearer to Mary and son

Ian that institutionalised fallacy was the order of the day. They heartily subscribed to it – until their lies hit the wall at the upcoming Local Court case to be addressed later.

5.2 Context for Concoction

The downmarket location suited an upset Mary. When an agitated Mary, accompanied by family members, arrived at the office of her legal aid lawyer, she found it to be located in a low income suburb with a high number of layabouts. This telling demographic signalled the site featured a high incidence of domestic violence. For this reason, the majority of cases that Mary's free lawyer dealt with were not civil family separation cases but criminal domestic violence cases. The lawyer's advice to Mary was tarnished by this professional bias.

Help was at hand. Conveniently for Mary, the lawyer's office was permanently graced with the presence of women's welfare workers who were pillars of strength to distraught victims of domestic violence. The welfare workers provided input into criminal court statements that typically involved medically treated physical injury for the woman and police custody for the assailant partner.

Their stereotypical perspective was a bonus. Mary purposefully refrained from attempting to change this entrenched monocultural image of a good-for-nothing wife-beater that her advisers held. She did not let it be known that Shaun was a mild-mannered scholarly professional, a slightly built 76 years old with heart and spine problems, was only slightly taller and heavier than her, and rarely drank alcohol. Mary and son Ian were pleased to be able to place outlier Shaun in the same boat as the socially undesirable scumbags familiar to their advisors.

The facilities in the lawyer's office suited Mary's mood to a tee. Her demeanour was shaped by a mix of three emotions: fury, at being threatened with ejection from her home (her expulsion loomed large), and unwanted legal action; fear, that her dream of 70/30 would not be realised; and resolve, to bolster her case in the Family Court so she could subsidize son Ashley's demanding lifestyle. Mary's rebuttal of Shaun's testimony went beyond genuine disagreement to fall outside the boundaries of fact, as she and eldest son Ian angrily rewrote history – something that will soon become apparent. That made her lawyer a partner in perjury. Mary was quietly pleased at the ease with which she was able to take everyone for a ride with her concocted tale of woe.

Mary had total faith in her advisors. The helpful women's welfare helpers added to son Ian's imaginative input, to put more meat on the bones of Mary's assertions of violence, mistress, and financial abuse. Her claims against Shaun were enlivened with rich input from their narrow monocultural perspectives, given their daily familiarity with vile acts of domestic violence.

The testimony being prepared was infused with vividly expressive embellishment from two specific sources. One was certification of Shaun's violence from a helpful 'Mission Australia', readily given just for the asking. The certificate was damning as it conveyed the impression that Shaun's violence was more proven than simply alleged. More important, Mary was armed with crucial material from the kind people at 'Women's Domestic Violence Advocacy Group' whose help she had sought when the court papers requiring her to vacate were served. There also the system had worked gushingly for Mary on the mere occasion of a request. The warm sympathy received from both organisations emboldened her to make assertions on the wild side.

As invective carried the day, restraint was a non-starter and temperance scarce. When it came to putting together her testimony against Shaun, Mary and son Ian saw little need to hold back. The inputs from the support networks and the lack of a guiding hand from her lawyer inspired Mary and son to go all out to say whatever they believed it will take to win the cases. The colourful content of Mary's made-up two-court testimony on her relationship with Shaun was to treat the courts to a feast of maltreatment accusations, cloaked in the deadly idiom of women's rights violations. If they were meant to cause Shaun mental torment, Mary certainly made her mark. Mary and son were unfettered by truth and in total disregard of exposure to ridicule in any future cross-examination, as will shortly become apparent.

In addition, mother and son needed to justify their condemnation of Shaun to the rest of the family and substantiate the fraudulent legal aid application being made at the time. As previously stated, Mary qualified for the aid by hiding from the aid agency Shaun's offer of an upfront payment to her of $20K, to project the false image of a penniless battered wife.

The idiom was mostly unfamiliar. Mary's statement ended up being framed mainly in the Australian vernacular, with touches of a colloquial street language that was essentially alien to her. The final product left her oblivious of nuances and therefore vulnerable in any future cross-examination – a possibility that never crossed her mind. Mary was glad to be able to defer to the verbatim input of the women's welfare helpers she leaned on because she was a migrant with limited knowledge of Australian culture and legal system, while her helpers were true blue Aussies with ample expertise in saving abused women.

Assessment of Mary's plethora of accusations against Shaun will need to be based on their *prima facie* credibility. That is enabled by the presentation of counterpoints from anticipated public cross-examination of her in the forthcoming Local Court case. That means pros and cons are juxtaposed to enable judgement on the believability of Mary's assertions against Shaun. It is not rocket science to see though claims that are patently illogical and internally inconsistent. All it takes is a modicum of intelligence for their far-fetched nature to be apparent. Mary's allegations will soon evocatively unfold. Readers will be left to make of it what they will.

There were three prongs to the attack against Shaun: domestic violence; keeping a mistress; financial abuse. We take each in turn, with the attendant commentary foreshadowing the public cross-examination of Mary in the Local Court case and, additionally, providing clues as to its strange ending.

5.3 Domestic Violence

The women's welfare worker helping Mary to draw up her testimony nodded in sympathetic support when Mary claimed she suffered 20 years of domestic violence. It was not one-off reactive violence, but systematic coercive violence involving serial assaults over that period. It was a humdinger of an allegation. The maltreatment could not have been worse. As far as Mary's helper was concerned, it was a sure-fire proposition – a certain winner because it was suitably grievous. The point was expanded to say that on the night before Mary announced her decision to separate, Shaun had straddled her in bed, pulled her by the hair and hit her, missing her face but striking her shoulder hard to cause her intense pain. She had tried to call the police but he had stopped her with threats.

When he saw the draft statement crafted with the help of Mary's advisers, Mary's legal aid lawyer did not ask her to explain why she had put up with such reprehensible conduct for decades, and even went to the four corners of the earth on prolonged travel involving 132 trips with someone so violent. That included weeks at a time, off the beaten tourist track, in remote parts of China and Thailand, where the police are not renowned for diligent policing of domestic violence. For the past nine years, Mary and Shaun would spend 5-6 months of the year with close family in her home country, where her brother, an influential police big-shot, had become husband Shaun's close buddy in recent years, having frequent social interaction and editing each others' publications.

To justify her inaction on Shaun's alleged abuse for 20 years, Mary took pains to expressly emphasise in the statement being drawn up that her family, including her policeman brother with a trained eye, knew nothing about the assaults etc until she told them on October 18 of that year when she pronounced her intention of leaving Shaun. She was not asked to explain how she was able to keep such a shocking thing a secret for 20 years when the family was closely knit, lived nearby, interacted often and spent prolonged periods together. Neither was she asked to explain why she did nothing to defend herself when Shaun supposedly straddled her, given his age of 76, slight build, heart condition, and back problem. Why did not Mary show her shoulder bruise to a doctor or have her family take her to the police? Mary was not required to explain as to why her son

Ian and others would drop her off to share Shaun's bed for two months – and that even after she had told them the terrible truth about his alleged violent nature. And that, moreover, was during a period when Shaun was being provoked without respite, day in and day out, by Mary's steadfast extortionist demand of refusing to vacate the sold property unless given 70 percent of the assets in the pool.

Most of all, Mary was not required to explain why she had tried to stop the sale of her home when its proceeds would have enabled her to escape the alleged misery. Why did she instead prefer the bewildering option of wanting to carry on with the allegedly horrid relationship?

But the violence allegation needed to be developed further. With helpful promptings from family, Mary spruced up her allegations of assault. That she did by stating that Shaun had, late one night, forced her out of the apartment in her nightie while she was under treatment for cancer, after asking her to leave behind the wig he had purchased for her. She had tearfully walked out on to the street bald-headed, where she sat on the pavement waiting for the police to pass by. After some time Shaun had dragged her back inside.

The line of thinking was way off beam. The alleged incident was a credible happening for the typical clients of Mary's women's welfare advisers, but made little sense in Mary's case. The deadbeat clients familiar to Mary's advisers lived in houses on the main street. But Mary lived in a luxury complex on the ninth floor with 24-hour security and in a suburban cul-de-sac. Had what Mary alleged actually taken place, the security guard on duty monitoring the corridors and lifts on CCTV 24/7 would have been obliged to call the police. The aftermath would have been Shaun's arrest and widespread gossip. Moreover, as Mary lived in a suburban cul-de-sac, the chance of police passing by was, unlike if she had lived on a main road, next to zero.

Apart from the above, Mary's lawyer failed to ask her why on earth Shaun would want her to leave late at night; and in her nightie. Had he been given to lashing out without reason in an alcohol-induced state? Or was it because he was off his medication for some sort of insanity? Also, as Shaun had bought the wig for her at a cost of $5800 and had it altered to suit her style, could he have, despite this, worn it himself if she were to leave it behind?

When Mary told her advisors that Shaun had repeatedly entered the sold premises while she resided there alone, they asked if he used to abuse her. When she said he did each time, but could not remember the words he had used, they mimicked the crude Australian lingo used by the drunken loafers with whom they were familiar: "Get out or I will smash your face in."

Shaun had no way to defend himself against this abuse allegation except to tell his lawyer that as a scholar and author the crude words attributed to him were foreign to his educated vocabulary.

There were several other petty complaints that left few stones unturned. Here are some examples. On being prompted, Mary claimed that Shaun controlled her. He did not let her drive his BMW even though she had never in her life held a driver's licence; he dictated to her what she should wear each and every time, although he never did; he prevented her from finding employment, a subject that never arose. Mary denied that she took most of the household furniture, electronic sewing machines, cutlery, and crystal ware from the family home, as claimed by Shaun. She said *he* took most of it.

If the above accusations tend to smack of the peculiar, the ones to follow would tend to be more on the side of the bizarre. While they are unlikely to be enough to cause the audience in the court theatre to fall about with guffaws of laughter during Mary's cross-examination, they may nevertheless have the potential to provide heightened entertainment for smiles up sleeves.

5.4 Mistress

There is nothing like a mistress to perk things up.

A mythical mistress was created. Being from an Asian country Mary thought it a great idea if, as is common for successful men there, Shaun had mistress. When she ran the allegation past her son and advisers they jumped at the idea, as a mistress would come in handy for explaining the missing money, alleged by Shaun to have been transferred to Mary's unemployable son, Ashley. After all, Mary could not deny she had received the fortnightly credits to her account for household expenses, as these were recorded in bank statements. What she did with all that money was recognised as a huge hole in her testimony.

Mistresses have the bad reputation of sponging off their married lovers. Mary conceded that Shaun transferred money to her in supplementation of her Centrelink part-pension, but disputed his claim that she paid most of the sum of $1750/month (in 2019 values) to her son Ashley. True, Shaun would credit the account she operated, which was a joint account with him. But after every such credit, every fortnight, he would follow her to the ATM and when she had withdrawn the money, threaten her, grab much of it away from her, and then send it to his long-time mistress. Mary stated Shaun had remitted the forcibly taken money to his alleged mistress for 12 years, with much of the money going towards the construction of the mistress's house.

That explanation contained two causes for gladness. Firstly, it implied Shaun had hidden wealth in the form of at least part ownership of his mistress's house. That meant he could more easily part with 70 percent of the disclosed asset pool. Secondly, it got Mary off the hook about the money allegedly transferred to son Ashley; it meant no money was ever transferred to Ashley as it had all gone to Shaun's mistress.

Mary alleged that Shaun's mistress was a widow by the name of Lisa. When living abroad, Shaun would spend weeks at a time with her.

Mary's lawyer unquestioningly accepted every word about Shaun's mistress at face value. He did not ask her why she had put up with Shaun's relationship with his mistress for 12 years. Also, if Shaun was going to send the money to his mistress, why would he transfer the money to Mary's account in the first place, then only to threaten her and forcibly take it off her in a public place, and not once but time and time again, every fortnight, for many years. And why, moreover, could he not have withdrawn the money himself using his own card, since the account Mary was withdrawing the money from was a joint account. Further, why did she accompany him on prolonged travel overseas, if he had spent all the preceding time with his mistress?

Shaun's lawyer Gianna was not amused by the mistress allegation. She immediately questioned him about it. He emphatically denied he had a mistress. He explained that the alleged mistress, Lisa, was a friend of them both, that she was 75 years old, and last he heard was ailing with arthritis and a broken hip. He had not met her face to face for 12 years, the last occasion being when he attended church in the company of Mary.

But Shaun's lawyer was still not satisfied and wanted to verify her client's denial. It was fact-checked by calling for his and Mary's passports for the past ten years and giving her clerk the task of verifying whether every overseas trip Shaun made had corresponding travel recorded in Mary's passport. Shaun passed the test. Lawyer Gianna also asked for Shaun's credit card statements to check whether his overseas expenses corresponded with the time spent abroad in various countries with Mary. He passed that test as well. The investigation included whether Shaun's and Mary's credit card transactions recorded in the monthly statements were intermixed by location on a day by day basis, thereby indicating Shaun was not in the company of anyone else on the day. That exercise to clear his name of the 'mistress' allegation involved legal costs in excess of a thousand dollars.

An insulted Shaun was quite annoyed. He asked his lawyer to demand from Mary's lawyer documentary evidence in support of their allegation of a mistress and payments to her. Despite reminders, there was no response from Mary's side. There was never any evidence whatsoever produced at any stage on that pernicious allegation. The thrown mud stuck nevertheless.

5.5 Financial Abuse

Using her third prong, Mary alleged financial abuse through financial deprivation and intimidation. That included not meeting her medical expenses, as certified by 'Mission Australia'.

Mary disavowed any benefit from her travels. She rejected as irrelevant all that expense by Shaun on extensive and prolonged overseas travel. The 132 trips included high-end foreign tours, cruises, and stays at beachside resorts, which were estimated at $810K for both over the period of the marriage in 2019 values. Also included were countless shopping trips to Asian cities where Mary was able to flash the cash and fill a suitcase or two. The purchases were mostly for herself and her family, all paid for by Shaun. Mary declared she went with Shaun as a favour to give him companionship on his business and leisure trips, so *he* owed her. No reason was given as to why, because of Mary's disinterest in travel, Shaun never once had his alleged mistress accompany him instead. Mary's lawyer had no problem with testimony that did not add up.

Mary's claim, backed by 'Mission Australia', that Shaun denied her medical treatment was contradicted by direct evidence. Mary's lawyer did not ask her to explain her allegation that Shaun had failed to meet her medical expenses, when there were receipts showing payments on Mary's behalf in the amount of some $8000 for medical gap payments over a three month period, just a year before the separation. The total sum paid for medical purposes and medicines over the period of the marriage was estimated from the discovery documentation to have exceeded $62K in 2019 values.

Mary alleged that her credit card was an instrument of control. When abroad Shaun paid for everything and, because of that, she could not use her credit card when travelling. The question was, since Shaun paid for everything, what was her need to use her card? Mary also alleged that Shaun discouraged the use of her credit card by demanding the slips for monthly checking. That limited her options to freely use the card and implied control. Mary's lawyer failed to note that she held a secondary card from Shaun, that her expenses were being paid by him, and that it was normal practice to check transactions against the monthly statement, especially when they had taken place abroad.

Another example of alleged financial abuse was, of course, Shaun's fortnightly forcible seizure of household money at the ATM for transfer to a mistress for several years, as described above.

As for Mary's overseas pensions, the mystery was finally over. Shaun had alleged that Mary's foreign pensions were hidden from him during the full period of the marriage, and not declared to the taxation office or Centrelink. He believed the proceeds were given to her son Ashley. Mary's written reply was that the pensions were a pittance averaging some $4000 a year for 20 years ($80K), and that it was all given to Christian charity. When documentary evidence was called for she said there was greater blessing from giving to charity anonymously, so there was none. The matter of the implied welfare and tax fraud was of no concern to the 'no-fault' Family Court.

Mary alleged that a property was transferred to Shaun's mentally disabled son to benefit his mistress. That she claimed was financial deprivation. Her lawyer did not question what she meant by that. The property was transferred to the Commonwealth government for no money (i.e. without consideration), to be held in trust for Shaun's disabled son under Centrelink aegis and pursuant to the Social

Security Act 1991. How on earth could that transfer have benefitted Shaun's alleged mistress? Yet Mary's lawyer signed off on the obvious nonsense. Mary's lawyer failed to note his client's household had benefitted from the property's rent for 16 years, until it was transferred to government ownership.

5.6 Verities & Balderdash

Information is power. So is misinformation, when it is accorded a legal forum by the Family Court, where it can stand unquestioned. And, moreover, stand pat in spite of it being formally rejected by another legal entity – *a la* the coming narrative in section 6.4. The failure of the Family Court to examine the truth in testimony before it is a laxity that seems to encourage the type of practice reported here. As will later become readily apparent, facts counted for little in the testimony submitted by Mary to the Family Court. Although highly questionable as just shown, the testimony still had enough oomph to move the needle against Shaun, by increasing its potential to prejudice the Family Court against him and cause mental torment.

The objective of Mary's testimony was: vilify to nullify. That involved choosing denigrating words to devalue Shaun's provable five-star generosity. Denial of the obvious is a classic symptom of Sociopathy. Mary gave no quarter or showed any sense of personal vulnerability in making false claims. The content of her testimony reflected Western and Asian cultures, with sociopathic overtones that denied it a moral compass. Consequently, the statement of testimony drawn up for Mary was studded with weak points.

A clear-eyed assessment was lacking. Mary's side was unconscious of the fact that the stereotypical templates used were self-defeating. Mary's advisers failed to tailor the concocted testimony to accord with her unusual high end circumstances – thereby undermining its plausibility. Also, Mary let much of her testimony be composed in the idiom of the Australian vernacular, including uncouth language alien to her – thereby reducing its trustworthiness to others and putting shades of meaning outside her ambit of comprehension. Further, her the-more-the-better thinking, intended to, in effect, throw as much mud as possible at Shaun, packed her testimony with umpteen trivial complaints – the scattergun approach increasing volume but reducing efficacy. Mary's lawyer failed to curb the legal folly of over-indictment.

Yet for all that, the above weaknesses did not matter. Although the holes in her hard-to-swallow declaration exposed Mary to the risk of damning cross-examination, that hazard was never of concern to her. For everyone on Mary's side, including chief adviser son Ian, lawyer friend Mr. Crack, her legal aid lawyer, the women's welfare networks, and the members of Mary's immediate family, cross-examination of her was unthinkable – simply not on the cards. What was on the cards was cutting and running. An inkling of the possibility of cross-examination and realization of what it involved, would have spurred immediate withdrawal of the Local Court charges by Mary.

The lawyers' styles contrast sharply. The approaches of the two lawyers in crafting client testimony were very different: Mary's lawyer did not consider any of Mary's outlandish allegations a bridge too far, whereas Shaun's lawyer practiced fact-checking to a fault.

Lawyers use the Family Court's 'no-fault' indulgence for tactical advantage. Lawyers who support lying clients automatically get the upper hand when cross-examination is not in prospect. Then, not only are the innocent parties defamed and mentally hurt by the vilification, but have in addition to incur legal costs to clear their name. Mary's sworn statement on the subject of Shaun's mistress, considered scandalous by Shaun, was never tested in any court, as her lawyer had cunningly anticipated. It had nevertheless served its ignoble purpose by putting Shaun on the defensive and cutting a damning image of him in the Family Court, besides stressing him out from a sense of outrage.

5.7 Local Court Succour

The Local Court case had significance in the lives of both parties. The seriousness of the foregoing allegations motivated both sides to seek manna of sorts from the anticipated outcome of the Local Court case.

The Local Court magistrate had become an agent of salvation for Shaun. The allegations made were so damning they triggered a determination in him to fight back; defend himself he surely must. No matter what people say about the presumption of innocence, restraining orders inflict harm even though provisional and the allegations therein baseless. The Local Court became a necessary forum to refute what Shaun considered were disgusting fabrications that impugned his character. Although initially revolted, the more he thought about Mary's accusations, the more he looked forward to taking her on. With increasing confidence he repeatedly met up with his barrister to report the many holes he saw in Mary's statement. The aforementioned counterpoints to Mary's testimony were among those prepared by the barrister for cross-examination of Mary at the trial – obviously unlikely to give her an easy time.

Unaware of Shaun's counterattack plan, Mary was also looking forward to the Local Court case. She and son Ian spent countless hours discussing the multiple vituperative merits of their testimony. It had been crafted and okayed by experts and would never be contested, they were made to believe. That belief had been reinforced by additional testimony. Over a month after Mary's police statement, Shaun's response to it prompted Ian and his wife to get in on the act and lay it on thick with hyperbolised hearsay in police statements as an afterthought. Such productions enabled Mary's position to transform from defensive to offensive and from reactive to proactive. No less important was the added benefit to Mary of being able to use still more invective to belittle Shaun's meritorious claim of generously funding her high-end lifestyle.

Winning was a certainty in Mary's mind. She called the shots; if she had not been confident of victory in the Local Court case, all she had to do was simply drop the charges. She had complete faith in her advisers' view that the seriousness of Shaun's maltreatment as claimed by her will give him no option but to cave in – he was a certain pushover. The anticipated Local Court victory was expected to automatically infuse credibility into Mary's Family Court testimony, as it was basically common to both courts. That she thought would boost her share of the asset pool on settlement. From Mary's standpoint, it was all hunky-dory.

But the unexpected happened. The strange outcome of the Local Court case took both sides completely by surprise. That will be disclosed in the following chapter.

***

Chapter 6

LOCAL COURT CASE: DRAMATIC SIDESHOW

6.1 Blazing Guns

The police statement was colourful. As previously reported, an infuriated Mary was metaphorically shooting wildly from the hip when she filed a complaint at the local police station on 22 January. Shaun was totally in the dark about it. Never in his wildest dreams did Shaun imagine that such thing would happen to him, as he had never in his life assaulted anyone – not even as a schoolboy, he told his barrister.

There was intemperate denunciation. The three-page police complaint alleged 20 years of physical assaults, one unleashed as recently as 18 October (about three months back), 12 years of supporting a mistress, and severe financial deprivation throughout the marriage. Mary's allegations of violence against Shaun had resulted in a provisional restraining/protective order (technically, a provisional Apprehended Violence Order or AVO) being issued against him. As previously stated, that restraining order thwarted the Family Court Order giving Shaun exclusive access to the sold family home – a restriction later removed by the Local Court on application. That enabled Shaun to act on the Family Court Order giving him sole access, so he could proceed to conclude the sale of the family home.

But other restraints remained. Shaun was not to contact Mary or approach her anywhere. Importantly, he was not to contact any member of her family either. Not that he was doing any such thing at the time.

Mary had cleverly pushed the envelope. Mary was well aware, when she asked for the restraining order, that Shaun had already stopped contacting with her for some three weeks. Also, he had not been in touch with any member of her family for three months, ever since she had told him not to do so.

Three downsides at the police station did not bother Mary. She was not taken aback when asked by the senior constable taking down her statement as to why, if things had been so bad, her family had not brought her around for a sooner complaint than on 22 January. Her practised answer was that since the last alleged assault on 18 October, she wanted to wait till after her colonoscopy on 28 November. As previously stated, she did not mention that it was Shaun who took her to the hospital for her colonoscopy on 28 November, before later driving her back to their apartment to give her post-operative care. While a lame excuse is better than none, it paled in relation to her failure to explain the near two-month delay between then the date of the complaint (22 January) – or the provocation from the serving of the Family Court papers for ejection in-between (on 10 January). She did not think it mattered when it was noted in writing by the senior constable taking down Mary's statement that the complainant did not exhibit symptoms of violence. Nor was she concerned that the senior constable had expressly recorded the absence of any supporting evidence. Although a doctor's certification of medical treatment for bruising, for example, would have been helpful, Mary did not regard the absence of evidence a major impediment to her strategy, as mere words had well served her purpose.

6.2 Delivery on Demand

The failure to arrest Shaun did not mean failure to care for Mary. The senior constable's questions to Mary and failure to arrest Shaun are suggestive of a degree of scepticism about Mary's complaints. While the extent of any doubts and qualms the constable may have held cannot be gauged, it is notable that she did not follow up on Mary's serious allegations of violence with the arrest of Shaun, as Mary wanted to happen. It is probable the senior constable's training aroused at least a sneaking suspicion she was being used as a pawn in a witch hunt. But smelling a rat does not help the cause of fairness when the constable's discretion is stymied by the detached rigidity of police procedure with regard to restraining orders.

It is seen to excel as a precautionary device. The current thinking is that issuing a restraining order is, on balance, safer for society than denying it. If a restraining order is issued against an innocent person, that person will be mentally hurt, but can contest the decision by appeal. On the other hand, if a restraining order is denied and the applicant is, as a result, physically harmed, that adverse consequence is deemed to be socially much less acceptable than the besmirched reputation of the falsely accused. The restraining order places the PINOP (the person in need of protection) in a position of strength over the defendant, as follow-up complaints, whether true or false, will carry a lot of weight.

In practice, restraining orders are usually issued for the asking. Consequently, they are wide open to abuse by the unscrupulous.

Automatic issuance can transform the restraining order from a device for protection into a device for attack. That means it gets removed from its intended purpose of providing protection against violence. When so converted, it can be used for tactical purposes of both a professional and personal nature.

A restraining order can be a professional tactical device. Some lawyers have a professional fondness for restraining orders as a matter of course, even against the innocent. Criminalizing the innocent benefits lawyers since it strengthens their hand against the opposition and, moreover, compels parties to the dispute to confine their communication to legal channels. The latter includes preventing direct communication between the parties for an amicable or quick settlement. That tactic was a dishonourable feature of this case.

A restraining order can also be a personal tactical device. Mary used a restraining order for bestowing on her four benefits far removed from its intended purpose of protecting her from violence:

- Firstly, it was to be an instrument of credibility. Since Mary had lied to her family to poison them against Shaun, cementing that break was crucial to ensure their continued support. It would be disastrous for her if they came to know she had pulled a fast one on them. In addition, the restraining order backed up her fraudulent application for legal aid that was being made at about the same time as she applied for the restraining order.

- Secondly, it was to be an instrument of prohibition. It would debar Shaun for one year from the sold property that he owned and was seeking access to, after having forcibly ejected Mary through court action.

- Thirdly, it was to be an instrument of gain. A successful court victory proving Shaun's violence would make the provisional restraining order permanent and bolster Mary's financial claim in the Family Court settlement.

- Fourthly, it was to be an instrument of revenge. False charges with malicious intent would transform a shield into a sword; Mary would be able to pervert a provision designed to prevent harm into one that inflicted harm. The restraining order would teach Shaun a lesson for having ejected her from the family home. It would prevent his access to it, vilify him, and have him arrested and jailed, as told to her would happen. Mary mentally pictured Shaun behind bars following her police statement, and so was surprised to see him standing in a bank queue the next day, completely in the dark about what she had done.

Automatism has the incidental effect of endowing restraining orders with omnipresence. Their ready availability enables them to reach into all family homes, to be a comfort or a threat, at all times. Their ready availability to persons with personality disorders, as was probably the case with Mary, makes them open to abuse, imbuing them with the capacity to deny partners their fundamental rights on the lines previously described in Chapter 4 and added to shortly in section 6.6.

6.3 Illusory Expectations

Mary thought the Local Court case would be plain sailing. Her sketchy grasp of the Local Court process was associated with a flawed calculus. She expected the Local Court to be there for her with a willingness that matched her easy wins against Shaun till then. Mere assertions against Shaun had worked smoothly in the past; so far it had been a proven normality for people to take what she said at face value.

For that reason, the Local Court case was seen as a formality. Mary was under the simple-minded delusion that the Local Court case would be more or less a rubber stamping exercise. She believed the purpose of the case was to put Shaun in the dock, have the public prosecutor publicly blame him and shame him before the family on the basis of her unsubstantiated assertions, and have the provisional restraining order automatically made permanent. It never crossed her mind the case would involve a formal trial where she and her son would be up for cross-examination over a period of 2-3 hours in the dock.

Expert help gave Mary a rash confidence. In deciding to proceed with the restraining order against Shaun, Mary was acting on mistaken advice given in good faith by her various advisers. The women's welfare helpers backed by her son Ian had made a special effort to draw up a damning case against Shaun. The professionals had ample experience and understood Australian culture and its legal system. They exuded a confidence about Shaun being found guilty that was catching. How could they be wrong?

There was no realisation the parallel was inexact. The problem for Mary was that, while her support network's assurance of success had been well meaning, it did not apply to Shaun. His case was not of the common-or-garden variety. In usual instances, when police complaints are made, some form of violence has actually occurred, almost always requiring medical treatment. In such run-of-the-mill circumstances, the motivation for the accused to want to go to trial to defend themselves at high monetary cost is zilch. Also, if the alleged assailant is in employment, there is added incentive to get it over with. Handily, the Local Court system gives alleged assailants an easy way out if the inflicted injuries are not serious. All they have to do is accept the provisional restraining order on a permanent basis without conceding that they did anything wrong. In these typical circumstances, a cave-in is a win-win.

That easy option was a non-starter for Shaun. Shaun's barrister, a leading light in Sydney, gave Shaun the option of accepting the restraining order without accepting as truth what Mary had said against him. Shaun angrily dismissed that easy option out of hand. He did so despite knowing that going to trial will cost him a hefty $15K and loads of stress. On the matter of domestic violence there exists concurrent jurisdiction between the two sets of courts. That means there is seamless articulation between the Family Law and the Criminal Law. Consequently, the Family Court usually regards the defendant's acceptance of the restraining order without admission as *prima facie* evidence of violence. There was no way Shaun was going to accept a restraining order for having done nothing wrong; he was going to fight till truth triumphed, no matter what it cost. Fight he bloody well will; never will he yield.

Shaun's barrister girded up his loins. At a third Interim Hearing, the magistrate in the Local Court, after examining the file, gave him four hours for the restraining order case at a Final Hearing on a date about two months hence. Shaun's barrister wanted to go the distance by performing the class act of incisive cross-examination of Mary. He was gearing up for flushing out the truth by discrediting what he considered were a litany of far-fetched, and even laughable, allegations. Mary's welfare advisers, having believed her, had not bargained for that. So their advice to Mary, although well-meaning, was wide of the mark and put her in quite a tight spot.

6.4 Pathetic Anti-Climax

What a letdown! After all the public resources expended over four months to protect Mary from danger, the Local Court, like the fabled mountain, laboured and brought forth a mouse.

It was over before it started. On the day of the Local Court case on 30 May there occurred at 10.40am the farcical spectacle of a baffled Mary, accompanied by her family entourage, dejectedly exiting the court premises. The blockbuster legal extravaganza, namely the case they had pinned so much hope on to give Shaun a public caning, and spent countless gleeful hours imaginatively discussing, was not, after all, going to happen – never ever! They were told the case was not going to be heard; it was all over. And they were told to go away by the public prosecutor, no less.

The Local Court flop was an unforeseen strategic setback for Mary and son Ian. But what they had lost owing to their botched strategy was only a battle in a war that continued. So there was no hightailing cowardly retreat. In fact, they still had Shaun in their crosshairs and spoke aggressively about other ways to skin the cat, even as they walked to Ian's car. Mary half-jokingly told son Ian that she should have inflicted a bruise on herself as planted evidence before she went to the police. The consolation for them was that, although the provisional restraining order was cast aside and the anticipated transformative benefit from this case to the other was lost, they had still inflicted damage on Shaun's reputation and wallet. They were pleased the provisional restraining order had disgraced Shaun for four months and expected the mud thrown to stick for much longer.

Before that morning's debacle, losing was unbelievable. When Mary arrived at the Local Court premises on 30 May she had been brainwashed by her advisers to believe victory was assured. Although surprised when told by the public prosecutor that she was going to be cross-examined if the case were to proceed, she lacked realisation of the true extent of her vulnerability from that exercise – her exposure to a roasting in cross-examination if that were to happen.

But the public prosecutor was an unacknowledged knight in shining armour. His grasping of the real McCoy saved Mary from the 'ordeal by fire' that awaited her in cross-examination, given that her testimony was riddled with inconsistencies and falsehoods. The public prosecutor had studied the file and found she had no case. There was no valid basis for prosecution. There were no grounds to believe that Shaun was a threat to her and therefore there were inadequate grounds on which to make the provisional restraining order permanent. The public prosecutor sternly advised Mary to withdraw the case and leave.

Shaun wanted the case to go forward. Shaun was unaware of the public prosecutor's retreat at the time. He was collectedly seated in the court foyer with his lawyers waiting for his case to be called. Strangely, he was actually looking forward to the case as a way of clearing his name. What on earth had he done to deserve such a disgusting criminal charge against him? He did not know at the time that Mary had met her Waterloo: an official rejection of her fallacious charges. Up to then no one had challenged her peddled lies; she had got away with repeatedly playing fast and loose with the truth and had been able to keep running red lights without penalty for more than six months.

After the public prosecutor had called Mary out on her complaint, there took place a strange happening on the court premises. It was said to be unprecedented because Shaun's barrister later told him he never before had seen such a thing happen. The public prosecutor sought out Shaun sitting in the foyer of the court premises, introduced himself as the public prosecutor, and shook Shaun's hand saying said he was not going ahead with the case. Shaun was nonplussed; stumped for words. Shaun managed to mutter to his barrister beside him that he preferred that the trial go ahead. The public prosecutor smilingly insisted there was no case to prosecute.

The case was thrown out. The public prosecutor invited Shaun and his lawyer into the courtroom and moved with undramatic bearing to request the magistrate dismiss the case. The magistrate hastily signed off on it, even before the public prosecutor was done addressing the court, dropping the case like the proverbial hot potato. There was a deafening silence on the matter of cost recovery. For fans of legal theatre eager for a rich performance, the court case was a dismaying damp squib.

It was an embarrassing *faux pas* for the police. Inside the court room waiting for her case to be taken up was the senior police constable who had taken down Mary's intemperate statement and warmed the cockles of her heart with a prompt restraining order against Shaun. Shaun noticed the policewoman was biting her lip during the dismissal of her case. Shaun wondered if she realised she had been tricked into letting Mary hijack the legal system for an unwarranted restraining order that demeaned its laudable purpose. To label a man who has never been violent as violent and impose a restraining order on him was, after all, not a nice thing to do. The restraining order contained insultingly stern advice to Shaun, offensively ordering him to seek counselling for his violent disposition on a presumption of guilt. To be the recipient of such a document was in itself disgusting. Shaun wondered if the senior constable would consider investigating Mary with a view to taking action against her for false charges, given that bogus claims dishonour genuine victims and the justice system.

The restraining order procedure had made subterfuge feasible. There is, as previously explained, an understandable mutual exclusiveness between the vital need to protect women from genuine violence and the common law principle of 'presumption of innocence.' Practical necessity requires that the principle be temporarily suspended even though it is an international human right under the UN's Universal Declaration of Human Rights, Article 1. Society dictates that it is better to be safe than sorry. But temporarily turning that principle on its head for valid practical reasons by the senior constable in this case shifted the burden of proof onto Shaun. That shift opened a treacherous gap in the judicial system. The resultant loophole enabled Mary to successfully exploit a public resource (the constable) for a private purpose (her revenge).

6.5 Unjust Ramifications

The smell of stigma lingered. Termination did not bring happiness for Shaun. Although the dismissal of the Local Court case freed him from its clammy grip, there was no cause for gleeful merriment.

Although vindicated, Shaun was shabbily treated. Despite the dismissal of his case, he had already suffered penalties without wrongdoing. He saw it as a frame-up for victimisation of the innocent. Though there was no proven culpability, Shaun was tarred and feathered by the besmirching of his stellar reputation. There was no mechanism for trashed reputations to be restored. No legal provision for a formal apology from Mary existed. That was besides the expense, stress, and disruption to life. Had he been in employment, his livelihood could have been threatened. The discharge of the case did not enable the recovery of costs amounting to $16K necessitated by the travesty. The dismissal of the case robbed Shaun of the opportunity of using the vehicle of a trial to publicly clear his name. Shaun felt letdown the trial was not proceeded with, yet relieved the pressure had eased.

Was there really justice? Being accused of violence is not the same as actually being violent. Yet can a restraining order on an innocent person for four months ever be okay just because it is provisional? Shaun had wasted money on a barrister who had come prepared to unpick Mary's tale of woe and lay bare the naked truth in cross-examination over 2-3 hours. Because Mary's claims had no basis, just contextualising them would have undermined them.

But Mary escaped unscathed. That was despite having sworn to baseless and patently implausible allegations. Many dangling threads were left unpulled to the benefit of Mary by her escape of potentially damning cross-examination. But Mary did not appreciate any of that because she had been brainwashed into expecting a pushover. Since revenge was justice for Mary, the Local Court outcome, far from bringing relief, was for her a setback. Her adventures in the arena of process abuse were brought to a sudden halt when the public prosecutor did the unexpected and rejected her sworn accusations. Her statement was probably considered too full of holes to pass the 'strategic deception' test.

Auxiliary facilities unwittingly fuelled Mary's vindictiveness. There were three institutional sources of support for Mary, besides her son Ian, whereas Shaun had none. There is no doubt that the social support networks are pillars of strength for the genuinely needy. However, they become anti-social instruments for unjustly walloping the innocent when exploited by hypocrites. Mary's abuse of them was no different to her abuse of the police and courts. It is a symptom of institutional weakness when facilities meant for good can be manipulated for ill, causing social help to inflict social hurt.

6.6 Causative Motives

Deeper questions arise. What were the motivational factors behind patently harmful practices?

Well meaning people in the support facilities were fooled into extending support to someone wanting to transform facilities designed to help distressed women into instruments for inflicting calculated harm on an innocent man. Why?

Mary played upon presumptions. A combination of self interest and self reference may explain well meaning conduct that was counterproductive – where a kind act to Mary empowered her to inflict deliberate collateral harm on the sinless.

For one thing, there is the compulsion of vested interest. Being used to dealing with genuine indictable cases of domestic violence, these support organisations would have a disposition to help everyone seen as belonging to the monolithic victim class. Domestic violence may even be seen as an intrinsic patriarchal phenomenon – a viewpoint that regards men as being violent by definition. Such affinity and beliefs can be expected to infuse accusations made by claimants like Mary with *ipso facto* credibility – loosely meaning, automatic believability. Also, it is elementary political science that institutions create vested interests that are by definition complainant-friendly. Reaching out to help is what they are there to do. Otherwise they would not be justifying their existence.

For another, there is the compulsion of empathy. Besides self-interest, there is also the concept of 'self reference' from several fields, including sociology. Self reference is when you believe the other person thinks like you; if you have suffered genuine violence, you have intuitive empathy for someone who claims the same. Then you are inclined to look upon that person's troubles as you do your own. Understandably, a soft spot from vicarious participation in another's emotions can trigger an outpouring of institutional support, without verification of veracity, just for the asking.

Arguably, Mary bit the hands that fed her. Mary was able to take the well-meaning people in the support facilities for a ride with a con artistry that took advantage of their trusting good faith. Donning the victimhood mantle hid her furtive motives of vengeance and tactical advantage, thereby tricking people who took her at her word. On a broader social level, there took place, yet again, penalty-free process abuse by Mary, but in this instance the abuse was of judicial support facilities rather than of the judicial system itself.

Once more, Sociopathy helps explain Mary's conduct. Sociopaths are empathy-free and have no respect for laws and propriety. Anger is their strongest emotion, with love and caring being shallow emotions. Mary's expulsion from the family home violated her sense of entitlement and triggered outrage. Since challenge and rejection can impel unconscionable reactions, they almost certainly explain Mary's merciless lashing out. Sociopaths are known to exploit court systems against opponents to make their lives a living hell.

There is strong reason to believe that some aspects of Mary's sociopathic behaviour are attributable to narcissism. Narcissism is a quality that can be associated with Sociopathy and is characterised by an exaggerated sense of self-importance. Grandiosity is the signature trait of narcissism. Since eldest son Ian was behind Mary's every move, he may also have been stricken with such anti-social personality disorder.

A ready falsehood is part of the narcissist's stock-in-trade. Because of a sense of greatness, narcissists would tend to think their word is superior; they are inclined to believe their pronouncements would be accepted as gospel truth simply because the statements came from them. Pomposity dictates that what they state must count more than for others. That aspect of Mary's, and perhaps son Ian's, personality disorder explains their intelligence-insulting falsehoods featuring outlandish assertions. The restraints of morality and mercy were in short supply.

Relatedly, narcissists covet others' accomplishments. What laypeople see as jealousy causes narcissists to believe those perceived as being better than them should be dragged down. Mary's, and perhaps son Ian's, narcissism explains why the judicial system was used as personal machinery by low achievers to cut highflyer Shaun down to size.

6.7 Process Abuse Fallout

We get down to brass tacks. Despite all that intervening drama, the police complaint that began with gusto ended in fiasco. The frustration felt by both sides by the dismissal of the case made them strange bedfellows. It was a deficient judicial system that allowed fake claims to go so far for so long. There had been much activity in regard to the Local Court case over a four-month period. That included several police statements, application of the provisional restraining order, its amendment, four court hearings, many pages of submissions, several consultancies with lawyers, and high legal costs. There were a whole lot of public and private resources wasted on Mary's personal mission, the charges brought not having a leg to stand on. To make matters worse, the Local Court sideshow added painful delay to the lumbering Family Court case.

The public prosecutor, like a legal Houdini, had waved his hand and made the case disappear. That enabled him to be spared a professionally embarrassing blooper, as the case would likely have been laughed out of court. He dodged a case that was preordained to be a loser on account of blatant perjury. Why on earth had he not opted for dropping the charges sooner, rather than wait four months for the day of the court trial? That shows up yet another procedural weakness in the judicial system and validates the maxim: 'Justice delayed is justice denied.' The public prosecutor's self interest saved the day for him, with a spinoff benefit that enabled Mary to escape a bad court experience. The public prosecutor let Mary get off scot free despite her contempt of the niceties of civilised life, or more to the point, contempt of the law.

The legally permissible was ethically reprehensible. Lax judicial processes set the tone for Mary's contempt of propriety. It enabled her to cross a red line with impunity and cock a snook at the judicial system. For Mary it was heads-I-win-tails-you-lose; once again she got a free pass and once again it was left for Shaun to pick up the pieces. Mary and son Ian had, by selfish exploitation of a lax judicial system, satisfied their craving for vengeance.

The dismissal of the case brought benefits to the prosecutor and Mary, but at the cost of pain for Shaun. His punishments came from the processes he was compelled to navigate up to the dismissal of the case. While wife Mary's accusations of physical violence were dismissed as effectively unfounded by the court, Shaun's accusation of psychological violence requiring medical treatment was easily provable, but no-one gave a hoot. The tiring process leading to Shaun's Pyrrhic victory in the Local Court case dissipated his resolve for the real battle in the Family Court case. Justice seemed ever less a rainbow worth chasing.

There was a double whammy for society. The same institutional failure precipitating the debacle and causing a waste of resources had also inflicted staggering unfairness on Shaun. That made inefficiency and inequity a corollary of process laxity that the judicial and ancillary support systems were incapable of either preventing or making amends for.

Loose procedures had allowed justice to haemorrhage for five reasons: firstly, an innocent person was punished by process; secondly, there was impunity for a cornucopia of false charges; thirdly, the conduct of lawyers violated their judicial duty; fourthly, legal redress was delayed four months by the public prosecutor's failure to drop charges earlier; fifthly, women subject to actual domestic violence and genuinely needing help had their cause sullied by bogus claims.

***

Chapter 7

DISCOVERY: PSYCHOLOGICAL WARFARE

7.1 Weapon of Discovery

Losing face prompted Mary to up the ante. Mary, accompanied by son Ian, went to the office of their new lawyer, referred to here as Dudley, in June. That was not long after the Local Court drubbing. They were worked up with an aggression meant to override that ignominy. They had somehow to make up for that humiliation by regaining the initiative. Discovery remained a handy means of gunning for Shaun.

The process of discovery presents an opportunity for attack. 'Discovery' refers to compelling the opposing party to disclose factual information relevant to the case. Mary had been made to believe that abusing the 'relevance' aspect by asking for the moon would exasperate Shaun - that is, drive him nuts. It was a diabolical strategy that Mary and son Ian zestfully pursued through their obliging lawyer.

Shrewdness was strength. Lawyer Dudley was much smarter than the legal aid lawyer he replaced, and that came with an enhanced streak of ruthlessness. He immediately recognised Mary's blizzard of allegations in her Family Court testimony as a tissue of lies that in any cross-examination will be a howling hit for the opposition. Mary's testimony to the Family Court comprised much of the same discredited material effectively thrown out by the Local Court. The end result of the Local Court case did not surprise lawyer Dudley one bit, as he was well aware he was dealing with people whose integrity left a lot to be desired.

Discredited testimony was not a disadvantage, though. Lawyer Dudley was unconcerned that Mary's trumped up charges in the Family Court, already rejected by the public prosecutor in the Local Court, will have any adverse effect on her in the ongoing Family Court case. As someone who played the system, he knew full well the Family Court does not care a hang about false allegations; there was not even the ghost of a chance of Mary being punished for perjury. The implication is that one can generally count on official impunity for perjury – and never mind the insulting slurs on a decent person or the washout of the Local Court case. Despite the Family Court procedurally providing a ready forum for perjurious attack, exoneration of the falsely accused by separating fact from fiction did not usually fall within its scope of concern – denoting that permissive 'no-fault' implicitly offers an open invitation to malign.

Client Mary and Lawyer Dudley hit it off. Dishonesty did not disqualify clients for lawyer Dudley. He had no difficulty about fighting for shifty people who, he knew from the rubbish before him, lied through their teeth. He undertook the case knowing he could use his client's deviousness vis-a-vis Shaun's integrity to his professional advantage. Brazen and unabashed falsehoods that could not be disproven conferred on him a coercive advantage. They would not be challenged yet served the purpose of prejudicing narrow-minded registrars and cowing the opposition. Adopting this untoward professional stance did not make Dudley a rogue lawyer; it was normal for family lawyers to routinely corrode the fabric of ethics. Lawyers of that ilk do not bother about the broader cause of caring justice, as will be diagnostically explained in the following chapter.

A new plan of attack was essential for lawyer Dudley. He wanted to downplay Mary's patently questionable testimony to the Family Court with a fresh approach that would overshadow it. Finding one was easy; discovery was a handy weapon of choice. In the meeting, Mary and son Ian suggested to Dudley two lines of investigation against Shaun that went the whole nine yards: firstly, look for hidden lucre by probing every nook and cranny of Shaun's life; secondly, somehow include the value of the property occupied by Shaun's disabled son in the asset pool. Both avenues of inquiry would slow-walk the case along a pathway leading to the Holy Grail of 70/30 settlement. That implies Shaun was in for a lengthy battle royal at great expense.

Client Mary's eagerness to find where the imagined bodies were buried suited lawyer Dudley just fine. The greater the volume of material sought in discovery, the greater the harassment of the opposition for softening their resolve, and the larger the fees flowing the lawyer's way. Since follow-up is possible, the process of discovery can have momentum from a feedback loop. A gung-ho driven harassment strategy was to deliver a package of benefits that was conveniently mutual for lawyer and client.

Discovery can be euphemism for intemperate psychological warfare. Unsurprisingly, lawyer Dudley used the weapon of discovery to pursue his client's objectives with hearty vigour. Abhorrence of bad faith was not a restraining factor. Shaun was required to disclose information in the hope of finding hidden assets that would justify his client's demand that exceeded the 50/50 already on offer. As in Pelion upon Ossa, the discovery process heaped harassment upon unfairness to make Shaun's life hellish. It involved a pernicious strategy, a merciless fishing expedition to weaken the resolve of Shaun and confer an undue advantage on Mary at the settlement hearing.

The contest in discovery was inherently uneven; what was maltreatment of Shaun was nothing much for Mary. While both sides do necessarily engage in the discovery process, the psychological war is usually not between equally strong combatants. The one with the greater assets becomes the bigger target; that is, the greater the assets, the greater the vulnerability to greater bullying. By implication, there can be no significant attack through discovery on anyone with nil assets. Consequently, Shaun with the greater assets suffered oppression relative to Mary, for whom discovery was close to being a cakewalk. The vast disparity in numbers tell you why: while Shaun submitted over 1500 pages of material for discovery, Mary submitted less than 20.

Mary was to yet again steal a march on Shaun. The very disparity in assets victimised Shaun; it punished him for being successful and affluent, while letting Mary off the hook because she had already secretly transferred her assets, and so had next to nothing at the time. The mismatched situation was yet another benefit to Mary from her long-term planning; that is, from having divested herself of assets in instalments before the calculated separation. Although the lopsidedness in assets skewed the process in Mary's favour and caused equity to go right out the window, it fell beneath the 'no-fault' Family Court's threshold of concern.

7.2 Pain of Discovery

Stealthy weapons inflict insidious harm. Abusing the discovery process to purposefully delay the court process can be advantageous to the disputant who is much more comfortably placed relative to the other. Because such purposeful delays from discovery can inflict significantly more suffering on the opposition relative to oneself, a contrived slow-walking of the case qualifies discovery as a sneaky weapon in a war of nerves in such circumstances.

Already acknowledged is that the speedy disposal of cases is not exactly a hallmark of the Family Court process. It was previously shown that institutional thrombosis in a congested Family Court system cripples procedural safeguards against unfairness in court processes. A second effect of congestion is scheduling delays in an overburdened court system. In this case, those backlog delays were further drawn out by additional delays from the filing of the Local Court case that mired the Family Law matter in the beleaguered Local Court system. The matter of the restraining order had to be decided in the Local Court before the Family Court case could move forward. These compounded court delays meant that additional delay from the discovery process would hold back Shaun's case even further, aggravating suffering because of his circumstances.

Delay imposed an unequal penalty on the parties; what was an inconvenience for Mary was an abomination for Shaun. Delay shunted Shaun into limbo, saddled with a case having an obscured timeline and an uncertain prognosis. Time was of the essence for Shaun because his life's savings were blocked, requiring him to live off loans. A once-affluent professional was forced to move downmarket due to the poverty of debt and reduced to a hand-to-mouth existence to which he was not accustomed. The doldrums had a groaning occupant for whom the pinch of hard times was a test of endurance.

By contrast, Mary's circumstances were relatively comfortable and time was less precious for her. She was living in a retirement hostel on a full Centrelink pension, with the part-settlement of $35K received in January deposited in the bank. The relative comfort of the parties can be illustrated as follows: while Shaun was struggling for months on getting the voluminous information demanded of him by the discovery process, Mary was holidaying overseas in her home country, being there as always for her brother's birthday, using the advance payment she had received from Shaun in January for high living.

That made unfairness integral to the process and inescapable for Shaun. Yet it was not something of concern to the Family Court. Because the case lumbered along for 16 distasteful months, several due to delays from the discovery process, but added to by scheduling delays in two courts, suffering was prolonged for Shaun. This delay ate away at his resolve to keep fighting the case, with yielding to the pressure being exerted by Mary and her son becoming an increasing temptation.

7.3 Discovery Rabbit Hole

Discovery delivered a heavy blow on Shaun. Mary and eldest son Ian were both pleased with heavy-hitting lawyer Dudley's launch of the discovery missive in such grand fashion. It was good to know their lawyer was no paragon of virtue; he passed their acceptance test when he showed no compunction about targeting the apartment occupied by Shaun's mentally disabled son, now owned by the Commonwealth government.

The oodles of requirements were bewildering and browbeating. The seven-page letter from Dudley to lawyer Gianna dismayed her and floored Shaun. It demanded copious amounts of information on hundreds of matters going back 22 years to investigate Shaun's past. It was a case of: 'lay bare every detail of your life to me.' That was in addition to the over 500 pages of information already submitted in response to a five-page letter sent by the previous legal aid lawyer, which also probed up to 22 years back. There seemed no time limit, or any other limit, to the information sought.

It was indeed a tall order. The information sought included details on Shaun's previous divorce settlement 22 years ago; information on five properties bought, sold and mortgaged, since that time; details on his five bank accounts for ten years; details of his three superannuation accounts over the 20 years of marriage; particulars of 49 cheque payments over 10 years; trip by trip information of his travels over 10 years; his credit card statement on six accounts over 10 years (some of which had been closed along the way); his Qantas frequent flyer statements for five years; details of insurance policies held over 20 years; statements on bank accounts that he had closed and forgotten about but details of which were supplied by Mary; statements from his publisher showing royalties paid on his books published and sold - and so on and so forth

The discovery demands included shooting wildly from the hip. That was because, among many other matters, Shaun was asked to prove negative facts. For example, he was asked to show that he had *not* supported a mistress and that he did *not* have hidden money overseas, when common sense dictates the onus should be on the accuser to produce some evidence to justify their allegations. Shaun was also dispatched on wild goose chases, being required to furnish information going back decades on bank accounts he had long forgotten about and properties sold he could not remember the addresses of.

In addition, the overreach in discovery was scary. It was numbingly dreadful for Shaun that the information required of him included details on the trust set up for disabled son Matthew, which was owned and operated by the government under Centrelink aegis. He thought that was inviolate; beyond the pale. The information wanted was the Trust Deed, Centrelink correspondence, mental health information, and the cash account statement showing monies spent for maintaining the son's apartment like strata fees, rates, repairs, and the like.

The discovery task was herculean. A job that was apt for a task force of forensic accountants was left to a lonely old man, aged 76 years, with a heart condition and no accounting knowledge. It was tedious, intimidating, and expensive. It took many weeks to do. Shaun's nerves were shot and he was close to breaking point; the thought of suicide entered his mind. The less-than charming use of the weapon of discovery by Mary and eldest son Ian had made its mark.

Drudgery for Shaun was holidays for Mary. Having received praise from Mary on his investigation of Shaun, lawyer Dudley told her she could now proceed with her long-delayed trip back to her home country to see her new granddaughter. Not much court activity was going to take place because his formidable list of demands was bound to tie Shaun up in knots for several weeks, if not months.

Vacation beckoned. Mary eagerly seized the opportunity to exchange the gloomy overshadow of the ongoing Family Court case for the sunshine of Asia. Besides seeing her new granddaughter for the first time, returning meant she could use her recently acquired wealth to entertain her friends and relatives to meals in the posh restaurants she and Shaun used to patronise, and update them on her divorce case. It gave her pleasure to use the social occasions to denounce Shaun for his alleged violence, mistress, and financial abuse even after the dismissal of the Local Court case, which was never mentioned.

Mary's story strained her credibility. Those who knew Shaun and regarded him a mild-mannered gentleman were sceptical. In fact, a psychologist friend who had met Mary in her home country rang Shaun to claim his intelligence had been insulted by Mary and accused her of narcissism. This professional diagnosis was later confirmed by Shaun's Australian psychologist, as reported in section 9.3.

7.4 Discovery Upshot

Discovery was a curate's egg for Mary. It yielded both counterproductive and triumphant results. Ironically, all but one of the shots fired at Shaun from Mary's discovery bazooka backfired to benefit Shaun and discredit Mary. Specifically, her claim of financial abuse by Shaun went up in smoke, as did her allegation about remittances to a mistress. Everything tallied and disproved her allegations (but did nothing to diminish the official status of her falsehoods, since they were allowed to stand unquestioned in the 'no-fault' Family Court). The documents asked of Shaun provided proof that Shaun had actually lavished money on Mary's travel, medical expenses, hairpiece, cosmetics, health insurance premiums, restaurant meals in Australia and abroad, telephones and the rest. Mary's lawyer recognised Shaun's documents as having general credibility but one exceptional vulnerability.

Lawyer Dudley told Mary they should concentrate on Shaun's Achilles heel. They saw that Shaun was most susceptible to attack in relation to what he had done for his disabled son. Mary heartily agreed. She and son Ian were adamant that disabled Matthew's trust assets must somehow be brought into the pool so Mary could reach her goal of 70 percent. They were quite unconcerned that their objective threatened the health and welfare of the disabled boy. Her lawyer, also focused on the same pot of gold, failed in his professional duty to warn Mary of the implications of what she wanted. Taking that amount of money would deny Shaun the ability to carry out his legal obligation to maintain his disabled son's property for the rest of the boy's life as required by the Social Security Act 1991 – implying future homelessness for his son. It is expressly laid down in the Trust Deed read by lawyer Dudley that the property should be sold if it can no longer be maintained. Hence, the sole bazooka shot to hit its target with deadly effect was the one aimed at disabled stepson Matthew's apartment.

While discovery equipped Mary's lawyer with a bazooka, Shaun's lawyer had only a pistol by comparison. Strangely, while Mary's lawyer was concentrating on Shaun's property transfer to his disabled son, Shaun's lawyer was not interested in the pension monies and house sales proceeds transferred by Mary to her able-bodied children. Lawyer Gianna's explanation was that all those money transfers were water under the bridge – that is, past occurrences that cannot now be undone or rectified. Since Shaun had lived with Mary for years while the transfers were taking place, it implied he had accepted them. That meant, according to Gianna, the transfers by Mary to her children over the years were not contestable, even though stealthily undertaken.

This argument lulled Shaun into the false sense of security about his disabled son's trust property. Surely, what was sauce for the goose was sauce for the gander. In any case, the property was transferred to disabled Matthew under Commonwealth legislation for a medical and welfare purpose. It quelled fears that had stalked him to that point. But he was badly wrong, as it later transpired to be highly contentious in a litigious manner. Shaun was unaware of the lurking horror, namely that that the Family Court registrar would not think on the lines Gianna had led him to expect. An unexpected turn of events enabled Mary to fill her boots while Shaun and his son got clogs. This asymmetry is of central focus in Chapter 9.

Shaun's lawyer concentrated discovery on Mary's current assets, specifically her overseas pension balance and her jewellery in an overseas bank vault – small beer compared to Shaun's assets over the years.

Mary repeatedly failed in her duty of discovery. And her lawyer subtly assisted in information suppression. While the information from Shaun violated his privacy by revealing his life to strangers, Mary's information remained mostly hidden and was never disclosed. Subpoenas could be issued to access Shaun's information but they were not available to get Mary's information. Aside from the fact that Mary had already divested herself of most of her assets, what assets she had left were in her home country, a foreign jurisdiction out of reach of Australian subpoenas.

The alternative to subpoenas proved ineffective. In lieu of the subpoenas, Family Court Orders were issued to the relevant foreign organisations, specifically the overseas banks and pensions department. But Mary used her considerable influence during her visit to her home country to pressure the recipients of Australian court orders to ignore them. They corruptly obliged. Yet again, Mary came out ahead, with Shaun getting the short end of the stick. Dishonesty proved to be the better policy.

All the aforementioned inequities were beneath the Family Court's radar. It has already been amply demonstrated that 'no-fault' as practised gives the green light to faulty practices of an unfair nature by clients and lawyers. The enforcement of procedural requirements ensuring fairness was more apathetic than zealous in the Family Court system. The remaining narrative tells you why.

***

Chapter 8

DICEY COURT SYSTEM: TOXIC INCOMPATIBILITIES

8.1 Fashioned Behaviour

The following reasoning sets the scene for the grand finale that is to follow in the next chapter. 'Caring' is recognised as the Family Court's signature attribute. A belief in the Family Court's professed caring mission, a calling that sharply distinguishes the Family Court from other courts, underpins the explanation presented here. An organisation's 'mission' tells stakeholders what it is *going* to accomplish, and is different to a 'vision' which states what an organisation would *like* to accomplish. The caring mission of the Family Court is expected to provide an institutional framework of values for guiding the conduct of those who participate within its enclaves. From society's standpoint, lawyers, registrars, judges, and other administrators are presumed to want to subscribe to the Family Court's caring mission, by tailoring their professional conduct to accord with its implied promise.

The focus in this chapter is on examining the institutional mechanisms – the constituent elements – driving the Family Court system. That is done by looking at the behaviour of disputants and lawyers on the one hand, and Family Court procedures on the other. These are of course related, as the nature and scope of player behaviour is enabled or encouraged by the court processes in place and enforced. Generally, when protective judicial procedures are not enforced, the standard of conduct of players can be expected to reduce, being fashioned by the broadened scope that the resultant process laxity enables. At its extreme, chronic process laxity can be expected to normalise corruption within the Family Court system.

Linkages determine performance. Understanding the interrelationships between process and conduct is a prelude to getting one's head around the baffling ending in the final act to be next presented. Only profound analysis based on actual experience can shine a light that is bright enough to penetrate the murky inner workings of the Family Court system. The illumination is expected to spotlight why the operation of the Family Court system flies in the face of its caring mission, by inflicting harm on those yearning for help.

8.2 Player Dramatics

The back story drives the fore story. Battles were won by Mary riding roughshod over procedural red lines. It was hard not to notice how harshly the weapon of discovery was used by Mary against Shaun, on top of a previous series of body blows. Mary's combativeness kicked off with extortion (using as leverage the illegal occupation of a sold property), followed by the countermanding of the Family Court Order (by making untrue allegations in a police complaint), then bringing unprovable charges in the Local Court to boost her claim in the Family Court (that was also an act of revenge for being evicted and the legal action against her, among other things), and finally using discovery as a weapon to weaken Shaun's resolve to resist (so he yields to a demand that will plunge his standard of living and threaten his disabled son with homelessness).

Lawyers are not expected behave like snake oil salespeople. They are expected to be a part of the machinery of justice. The three culprit lawyers in the case did not appear to have heard of *noblesse oblige* – that is, with position comes responsibility for moral uprightness. They failed to stand back and take a professional view of the situation with integrity. They did not perform in accordance with their assumed duty to society, the rule of law, or the caring mission of the Family Court.

Lawyers were in lockstep with Mary's malevolent shenanigans at one time or another. Mary's demands, despite their excessive and hurtful nature, struck responsive chords in her three successive lawyers. Responding to such demands was made easier by the leniency from process laxity in the Family Court, where unenforced rules permitted stealthy moves. Mary's lawyer Dudley was past master of the dark art of the classic fudge. He repeatedly demonstrated his experience in cunningly playing the procedurally weak justice system. His repertoire included, besides the heartless streak in relation to the disabled, ducking, weaving, and stonewalling. Mary's lawyers were complicit in the crafting of what was later shown to be a perjurious load of piffle. Also, they were party to a cover up in discovery. Lawyer Dudley provided a smokescreen for Mary's falsehoods and supported various attempts at burying the truth.

All of Mary's lawyers played a dark role. This they did by the fault of omission, namely failing to counsel Mary in the direction of fairness and justice. It is true that Mary had a bee in her bonnet and that what she lacked in integrity was made up for in determination. Mary's three lawyers knew that not only had Mary concocted much of her sworn testimony to the two courts, but also she had been less than frank with them in face-to-face conversation. They were well aware that Shaun's contribution to the marriage was extraordinary even as Mary underhandedly milked the relationship.

Guidance was lacking. At no stage of the process did lawyers advice an emotion-driven Mary about the unfairness to Shaun and his dependant son by her taking over 70 percent of the superannuation savings of a 76 year old man. Despite knowing the type of person they were dealing with, all of Mary's lawyers shied away from questioning her excessive demands and got the job of representing her by aligning themselves with her obsession of targeting a disabled person's sanctuary. And most important of all, they did so knowing full well that their success on her behalf in the courtroom would have the obvious knock-on effect of bringing devastation to innocent lives, one of whom was a disabled child – a helpless third party.

That blockbuster point might well typify professional deficiency. Although Mary's lawyers acted independently of each other, there was astonishing professional groupthink on Mary's unconscionable objective. When lawyers support malevolence, they must surely own malevolence. Such official conduct appears to flourish within at least some parts of the legal profession – and that despite failing to give objective advice arguably being nothing less than a failure of duty. If so, Mary's lawyers were untrue to their professional calling for justness and contemptuous of the Family Court's professed caring mission. Reported previously were monstrous lawyer antics that included complicity in, or tolerance of, extortion, perjury, breach of the Family Law Act, breach of contract, illegal occupancy, and the concealment of truth. Such a bundle of behaviour hardly qualifies relevant lawyers for a 'good performance' medal in a truly caring Family Court.

Gamesmanship of the Machiavellian sort thrived. The culprit lawyers routinely sailed close to the wind, churning up the blame game for their living. That implies they habitually sold their soul for the purpose. But that is no big deal; it should not flummox anyone that such lawyers can sleep easily in their beds after committing ethical sins of a cardinal nature. That is because their behaviour is based on an important truth. Such behaviour is not difficult at all when the hostile adversarial culture spawned in the Family Court system makes skulduggery normal. Lawyers are desensitized to the devastation caused to the innocent by the victory they seek. That would explain the absence of fitful sleeping for artful lawyers like Dudley, for whom winning was everything.

But let us not tar all lawyers with the same brush. The aforementioned conduct throws into sharp relief the principled behaviour of lawyers like Shaun's lawyer Gianna. When Shaun was unfairly treated by the opposition she told him she was not into tit-for-tat, even though she said it happened a lot. She performed the class act of meticulously checking on Shaun's testimony to ensure it was a declaration of truth. She pressured him into delivering on discovery although she recognised the demands were way over the top. Gianna's relative mildness and correctness, in the face of opposition aggressiveness and impropriety, disadvantaged her case. What follows throws more light on why, within the Family Court system, human decency is a generally unappreciated quality.

8.3 Theatre for Impropriety

Fishy ploys unfairly tilt the scales of justice. The harsh world of an adversarial system in full swing makes nonsense of the Family Court's professed caring mission. There appear to be chronic failings in unfettered adversarial and discovery processes when lawyers can be used as hired guns to criminalize the innocent and torment people who they know full well are estimable citizens.

Who dares wins? A self-serving belligerency emerges as the quality needed to win in the theatre of the so-called 'caring' Family Court. For example, Mary's lawyer was a predatory hunter-gatherer in stalking Shaun as prey. This he did by requiring voluminous information on 28 accounts and legal documents going back up to 22 years – well beyond of the six-year statute of limitations. One or more of the following hardball strategies can present itself as a winning prescription: 'dog eat dog;' 'might makes right;' 'anything goes;' 'everyone for themselves;' 'at each other's throat;' 'kill or be killed;' 'eat or be eaten;' 'survival of the slickest.' When this type of culture permeates an environment where procedural protections are watered-down, reasoned calculation for an amicable settlement understandably takes a back seat. Then, having been put through the mill, parties to the dispute are no longer in a mood to be nice. The added fuel to the fire better positions lawyers for improvement in fee-generation.

But do lawyers really deserve blame? Playing devil's advocate, we may say that a family lawyer of the Dudley sort, as the public's favourite bogeyman at the receiving end of curses, may be getting an unfair share of damnation. Arguably, such types are simply making rational responses to distorted incentives. If they are cruel to who they know to be decent folk suffering in unfortunate circumstances, it is because the Family Court system requires them to be heartless for professional success. It might be too much to expect lawyers to sacrifice their livelihood on the altar of ethical conduct. Lawyers, like physicians, cannot be expected to heal themselves. If so, that must surely highlight serious deficiency in the Family Court system promising caring justice.

That home truth enables one to hone in on the nub of the issue. The culprit elephant in the room is (you've guessed it): process laxity in the judicial system. Slack processes in the Family Court judicial system that denies procedural protection makes propriety optional in several regards. 'No-fault' can then be euphemism for slipshod practices. As the cat's away, the procedural leniency enables the adversarial system to advantage those who are less scrupulous at the expense of those who play by the rules. Relatedly, there is more money to be made in combativeness than in amicable settlement. Expecting ambitious lawyers driven by the imperatives of competition not to exploit the repertoire of improper opportunities offered by lax Family Court processes is absurd enough to make a dead cat laugh. And that pathology from laxity can extend to pre-trial processes, including the make-or-break Conciliation Conference. Overall, the fluidity in process laxity gives rise to connotations of quicksand for fairness. That makes procedural laxity by design, as seems to presently exist, an altogether bad idea.

But there is something else that is no less troubling, if what is plainly evident is anything to go by. Chillingly, the permissiveness in process laxity characterising the judicial system appears to have degenerated into licence. Specifically, that refers to the licence to violate human rights with impunity. Here are the more flagrant examples from the foregoing narration: the Family Court's inattention to extortion; the preparedness of the Family Court to take formal official notice of adverse Local Court findings against respondents (defendants) but ignore favourable outcomes; the Family Court allowing to let stand before it without demurring testimony dismissed in the Local Court, including blatant perjury; inaction on the leaking of confidential testimony in breach of section 121 of the Family Law Act; the four-month delay in dropping the Local Court case by the public prosecutor. Slated to come are the following likely bad examples from the forthcoming narrative on the Conciliation Conference: turning a blind eye to tactical late filings; not giving reasons for registrar determinations; the disregarding or discounting of obvious duress, contrary material facts, unequal contributions, conflicting Commonwealth laws, future responsibilities and needs, documented mitigating factors – among others.

Licentiousness implies the disregarding of accepted rules and standards – that is, contempt of fairness and decency. In Chapter 1, the milder definition of a Kangaroo Court was a court not observing recognised standards of law and justice. It is logical and natural that loose processes will offer opportunities for the less scrupulous to ruthlessly exploit as vividly illustrated in this tale. It is a sure thing; there is inevitability to it. What can you expect from a pig but a grunt?

That makes bad behaviour a symptom of a disease rather than the disease itself. The disease is institutional impairment in the judicial system. Impairment from the disease of laxity in court processes necessitates and facilitates dubious conduct in the judicial system by disputants, lawyers – and even registrars, as will soon be dramatically demonstrated. Unsurprisingly, the indulgence inherent in the 'no-fault' basis fails to pleasingly accord with the decorum required for credible justice.

The all-important conclusion that underscores the above information is as follows: if the Family Court players have not been living up to the expectations of society, it is more a reflection on the malfunctioning Family Court system than on the players.

8.4 Readied Stage

The preceding sobering analysis throws up the following compelling deductions.

When money is being paid to be adversarial, there is motivation to be adversarial for adversarialism sake. Adversarialism breeds adversarialism for indefinite self-renewal. That implies: the created vested interest in belligerency acquires title to future possession of the status quo.

The reasons for unfairness in the judicial system are by now plainly visible. Mismatched elements can interact to cancel out desirable authentic justice and deliver deplorable rough justice. Forces within the Family Court system are seen to be operating at cross purposes. The three components, namely the 'no-fault' basis, process laxity, and adversarialism, are key elements inherent and pervasive within the Family Court system. Although joined at the hip, they are mutually conflicting. Since they clash and lack congruence, they interact self-defeatingly to inhibit or deny the hoped-for caring benefits of 'no-fault.' In a sense, looseness in process allows the strife in adversarialism to suck the oxygen out of 'no-fault' and threaten the paradigm of real justice. It needs no longer be mysterious that the mutual antagonism in this tripartite institutional mix synergises in deadly fashion to wreak haunting unfairness of the type brought to light in this analysis.

What is more, there appears to be a doom loop. That is because the elements giving rise to rough justice are able to feed upon themselves for their indefinite self-renewal. As was stated, adversarialism has a life of its own, there being vested interest in combativeness. In addition, the 'no-fault' basis gives rise to process laxity that encourages adversarialism that in turn works to inhibit 'no-fault' performance, the impairment being hidden by lax processes - and so on. That is suggestive of a spiral of dysfunction. These arguments show there is self-perpetuation of defective mechanisms in the Family Court judicial system crying out for healing reform. The matter of how a malfunctioning Family Court justice system can mend its sinful ways is addressed in the final chapter.

The stage is now set for the grand finale happening in conditions where chronic malady is a habitual offering. Made known next are the inner workings of the Family Court's decision-making process as it applied to this case. There the curtain is brought down on the Family Court's 'no-fault' silver bullet solution to this pathetic relationship-breakdown problem.

***

Chapter 9

CONCILIATION: LET US PREY

9.1 Step-motherly Overreach

This section is precursor of the judicial outcome at the pre-trial stage. The following background information is crucial for properly understanding the legal strategy adopted at the final stage, namely at the Conciliation Conference, that brought about the baffling outcome in this case.

A property transfer was the bugbear. The fairness in the final judicial outcome hinged on Mary's demand for compensation on account of Shaun having transferred a property to the government to be held on behalf of his disabled son, Matthew. If Mary had not been hellbent on having the value of the transferred property included in the asset pool, the case could have been resolved amicably within a month of initiation and saved much of the legal costs of $65K for Shaun and $25K for Mary, besides the mental stress. Instead it dragged on for 16 months, driven by Mary's and son Ian's pathological obsession to somehow include the trust property in the asset pool.

Mary entered the relationship with her eyes wide open. She knew full well that Shaun had a partially dependant son at the time of marriage. Shaun's son Matthew was incarcerated in a mental institution with the disability of Schizophrenia at the time. Matthew was undertaking a university music course in jazz when he was struck by the illness. After Matthew was released from the mental institution, he was living on the street when he asked his father to find him a place to live. A two-bedroom apartment was hurriedly purchased in Adelaide, seven months into Shaun's marriage to Mary, out of Shaun's superannuation savings brought into the marriage.

The property generated rental income to Mary's household. That was the case for 16 years until transferred to the government. Matthew, on a disability pension, paid market rent to his father and stepmother, using a rent allowance received from the social welfare agency Centrelink as part-payment. Despite this income benefit to the household, Mary silently resented the purchase of the apartment for Matthew.

Stepmother Mary also disliked the attention Shaun was paying his son. Mary knew Shaun loved his son because of his almost daily phone calls, even when travelling overseas, his monthly visits to Adelaide sometimes with Mary, and his readiness to be at hand should his help be needed.. Mary complained to a mutual friend about Shaun's daily phone calls and was told it was natural and understandable. In fact, the friend asked Mary how often she spoke with her own several family members, and whether it was less than Shaun did with his only child. Mary did not like Matthew although he was always polite to her and unfailingly sent her a card on her birthday and even on mother's day. In fact, Mary harboured a hidden dislike for the boy even though he was always respectful towards her, being kindly and soft-spoken by nature. She certainly felt no sympathy for his condition. Her deliberate targeting of him in her court strategy publicly exposed, for all to see, a classical step-motherly dislike.

The property transfer by Shaun bestowed benefits of both a private *and* social nature. The private beneficiaries were Matthew and his father, and the social beneficiaries were the welfare services and the public mental health agency. If Mary had loved Shaun, his peace of mind from the property transfer would have benefited her also. Twelve years into the marriage Shaun was informed by a lawyer friend that there was provision to transfer his son's home to a Special Disability Trust under aegis of the welfare agency Centrelink, pursuant to the Commonwealth Social Security Act 1991. At that time, Shaun was having a relapse of his heart problems, and the mental health agency had notified him that his son would have been living on the street if not for the accommodation security he had. That accommodation security was crucial to Matthew's mental health and general wellbeing was confirmed in writing by the mental health service and accepted by Centrelink, also in writing. But all that written certification did not seem to count for much with the registrar in the Family Court proceedings, as will be shortly shown.

The property transfer process was protracted. After complex and long-drawn-out bureaucratic machinations over three years, Centrelink finally approved the transfer of the apartment occupied by Matthew to the Public Trustee (the government) without sales proceeds (free-of-charge). The Public Trustee was to own the property (have title) on behalf of Matthew for the rest of his life in a Special Disability Trust under regulations defined by the Commonwealth Social Security Act 1991. The transfer process required the services of a lawyer in another city. Apart from not bringing in sales proceeds, the process cost a lot, and included the payment of legal fees and stamp duty.

On transfer, the property transformed from an asset to a liability. Although the property was to be owned and managed by the Public Trustee, Shaun nevertheless still had responsibility under the Commonwealth Law for meeting its annual maintenance costs, including strata fees, rates, taxes, repairs, and the like for the rest of Matthew's life. He had responsibility to maintain it without sales proceeds or rent, out of his retirement savings. The Trust Deed specified that if the property was not maintained, it was to be sold. That makes clear Matthew had a legally defined dependency on his father for accommodation crucial to his health and wellbeing.

Mary and son Ian targeted Shaun's most vulnerable spot. With the support of three lawyers they reached a new low of depravity by threatening a disabled third party with future homelessness. Mary knew perfectly well that Matthew's apartment was much more than his home. It was a sanctuary that he had suitably darkened to suit his condition. It was his therapeutic hideaway monitored by mental health professionals. It had prevented his further incarceration or living on the street. This information had documentary support on file.

The responsibility to a dependant was subverted. Shaun had set aside $90K from his superannuation savings for maintenance of the property till Matthew was aged 80 years. But that did not seem to count for much with the registrar presiding over the Conciliation Conference. Shaun's legal obligation and the importance of housing for Matthew's state of health did not influence the final outcome. The money set aside for the property maintenance was lost to Mary.

But it may have happened for good legal reason? Readers will be left to make up their own minds on the merits of the outcome in the light of the cascading information featured in the following chapters.

The court theatre will feature a cast of five characters. They play distinct roles in the final Conciliation Conference scene, even as the proverbial fat lady gargles her throat in preparation for her song: upbeat Mary, enfeebled Shaun, shrewd Dudley, hamstrung Gianna, and a rookie registrar.

9.2 Self-Assurance

Mary was riding high when settlement was nigh. She was brimming with confidence when, accompanied by family members, she met with her lawyer Dudley in preparation for the final hearing – the Conciliation Conference. She laughingly noted her upper hand from having gamed the system with impunity, regarding it as a badge of honour.

Lifting her spirits for a happy ending were the assurances from her clever lawyer. Dudley shone for Mary with a pleasing ruthless streak that he demonstrated in going after Shaun in the discovery process and, more pertinent to the matter in hand, his readiness to do the same with regard to disabled Matthew's property in the final settlement. His lack of compunction in targeting that second property gave Mary and son Ian confidence they had in fortunate partnership latched on to a winner. Psychologically, Mary was thinking positive and was confident she already had victory in the bag. So when Mary arrived at the courthouse on settlement day 31 March at 9.30am for the Conciliation Conference, she was full of beans and fighting fit.

The interim had been annoying for Mary. It was now 16 months since her bombshell announcement to Shaun of wanting to separate without legal action. It had been a period not altogether to her liking. She was angered on discovering that her elaborate plan for easy money from extortion, the whole basis of her strategy for separation without going to court, belonged in the illusory domain of cloud-cuckoo-land. Further, she had been compelled to get documents on matters kept hidden throughout the marriage, particularly about her foreign pensions and bank vault contents. That had been an irritating inconvenience. She had also been made to run around in her home country to bring influence to bear that would neutralise the Australian court orders to banks and the foreign pension department. She had to confess to the Family Court about breaching section 121 of the Family Law Act by conveying confidential court testimony to Shaun's former wife, after having at first lied about it with the support of her lawyer. It was to be her one and only 'come-to-Jesus' moment. That was embarrassing. Although it was a humiliating admission, it proved no big deal in the end. Mary was not even admonished for violating the law by the friendly 'no-fault' Family Court, and the transgression was to count for nothing in its final reckoning.

Mary was comfortably placed. She was settled in a hostel, experiencing growing savings from the Centrelink age pension even after funding unemployed son Ashley's high-end lifestyle. Most of the money from the advance payment from Shaun was still sitting in the bank. The money she would get from Shaun in settlement was earmarked for her children and grandchildren from her previous marriage. She was conscious of eldest son Ian's desire to purchase a luxury car. The worst possibility was settlement at a cool 50 percent of total assets, an offer that was already on the table. That would give her more money than she ever had before, enabling unemployed son Ashley to be set for life and benefiting her six grandchildren, the apples of her eye, besides funding the luxury car purchase for eldest son Ian. But her hankered-after jackpot was settlement on a 70/30 basis – a bonanza beyond belief.

Mary was pleased that she had softened up Shaun ahead of the case. She suspected he was blind to the Belshazzar-style handwriting on the wall about his upcoming fate. She knew lawyer Dudley had a card up his sleeve that all but guaranteed such a result. She just could not lose.

Only one thing bothered Mary on the day. She was embarrassed to face Shaun after all the trouble she had caused him. In her heart of hearts she knew she had done him wrong; in fact, she knew she had gone overboard, blinded by anger at the time, but no longer. She had flashes of regret about what she had done to Shaun, but these were suppressed with rosy thoughts of the prospective riches coming her way.

Mary made a request through her lawyer to the court that she be spared the discomfiture of having to meet Shaun face to face in the courtroom.

9.3 Craving Liberation

In contrast to Mary's buoyancy, the clock was ticking for Shaun. With minor exceptions, Mary and son Ian had Shaun over a barrel for the duration of the case. Shaun was at his wit's end by the day of the final hearing at the Conciliation Conference on 31 March.

The offer to Mary was pruned. Shaun's lawyer Gianna was now offering Mary 40 percent of the total asset pool. It was down from the previous offer of 50 percent because she said Mary had failed to contribute to the marriage, but instead milked it for its duration. And Mary had done so at the same time as Shaun had lavished on her a dream lifestyle. But in retrospect Gianna's new approach amounted to nothing more than rearranging the deck chairs on the Titanic.

Shaun was fed up to his eyeballs. Yearning for his liberty, he was prepared to give 50 percent to rid himself of the damned case once and for all. Besides shackling him personally and financially, there was the deadweight of bloated legal debt nearing $65K. He had had enough; his life was in limbo, his loans-based existence was hand-to-mouth, the prognosis of his case was uncertain and, adding to his misery, was a recent warning about his health. About a month before the final hearing he had been rushed to hospital emergency by ambulance, and was diagnosed as undergoing a nervous breakdown and at risk of a heart attack. He was referred to a psychologist and was on medication for these conditions when he went to the Family Court for final settlement.

Shaun believed there had been a loving relationship for most of his marriage. Mary had never before shown the bad side of her character till her secret support of her youngest offspring, son Ashley, was objected to by Shaun. That milking had provided supply for fueling the relationship for its duration. Mary's worst demons were released following her ejection from the family home. Shaun realised the good times will never be back; the carnival was indeed over.

Psychotherapy helped relief replace regret. Relief from being single came to Shaun after he was informed by his psychologist that Mary appeared to exhibit the classic textbook symptoms of a sociopath. Shaun's psychologist told him what she regarded as common knowledge in the profession. Those afflicted by Sociopathy will dispose of anyone who gets in their way and take extreme vengeance on those who reject them. The condition is said to be associated with shallow favourable emotions and strong sex drives.

The penny dropped. It finally dawned on Shaun why Mary had done what she had done. Although disturbing at first, the explanation became increasingly therapeutic as it soothingly sunk in. The enlightening insight from the psychologist's telling words extricated Shaun from the needling perplexity of why Mary had done the unimaginable. In addition, the diagnosis serves to explain audacious process abuse. There was behaviour so outlandish as to fall between the cracks of a lax judicial system and its social support facilities.

Shaun now saw his suffering as a self-inflicted wound from marrying a sociopath. He knew financial settlement would capture supply for Mary and render him disposable. But be that as it may, settlement on that day at the Conciliation Conference was his hope of escaping what he had come to regard as the harrowing shackles of entrapment.

9.4 Baffling Outcome

Registrars are trained lawyers who hold the judicial reins at the pre-trial stage. Those court officers substitute for judges at the less formal stage of conciliation or settlement through negotiation between lawyers. They are in the vanguard of the Family Court process. The overwhelming majority of cases that come before the Court are disposed of by them without a court trial. The pre-trial stage is the centrepiece of the Family Court system where registrars hold sway. Their conduct overwhelmingly determines the quality of the Family Court's overall judicial performance. Under the Family Law conciliation rules, the registrar's views are not a judicial decision but a recommendation for consideration by the parties. Theoretically, the registrar's determination can be rejected, in which event the case would proceed to trial.

The Conciliation Conference on March 31 featured a registrar who was recently appointed. The registrar had replaced the previous one who had dealt with the case from the beginning. Mary's lawyer Dudley used a one-size-fits-all stereotypical script in stating his case.

In order to do so, Mary's lawyer played the 'comfort zone' card. The comfort zone is a psychological state in which a person feels comfortable because matters are within their ability and experience. According to psychologists, the comfort zone concept recognises the human tendency to prefer the known to the unknown (White 2009). That implies an instinctive aversion to novelty including, in this instance, to cases with unusual features like a Special Disability Trust in conflicting Commonwealth legislation. Dudley forced the facts of this unusually complex case into a standard framework, by not referring to the complicating factor, namely the Special Disability Trust and the conflicting Commonwealth law underpinning it.

The final hearing at the Conciliation Conference on 31 March began on a sour note with Mary's lawyer wrong-footing the opposition. The registrar was made to put up with a commonly practised dirty trick. Lawyer Dudley made a late, last minute, filing of Mary's court documents. This wily tactic handicapped Shaun's lawyer Gianna, as it denied her the time to study the opposition's position. That caught her on the hop and contributed to an outcome lurking around the corner that ended in tears for her side.

Shaun had faith the registrar had done her homework with sufficient diligence. That would make her aware of the contents on file and be alert to the lack of straightforwardness in the case. He assumed she would take all material factors into account and not be misled by lawyer Dudley making a drama of issues, his crafty use of red herrings, and his suppression of information relating to the Special Disability Trust and other Commonwealth law.

The stereotypical script carried the day. Currying favour with an ingratiating tactic, lawyer Dudley presented a one-dimensional argument which typically applied in Family Court cases. He skirted the messy wider context about the Special Disability Trust etc, which was nevertheless recorded in court documents. Knowing the quick-fix disposition of Family Court proceedings, Dudley went for the jugular by targeting Shaun's disabled son Matthew's property with a standard argument in a non-standard case. His argument was based on the Family Law requirement that all property transferred during the course of the marriage is material to the settlement, regardless of reason or purpose.

Dudley claimed he had incriminating evidence. Crucially, he stated there was evidence of intent on the part of Shaun to deny Mary the value of the transferred property. He produced a cheque issued to a family lawyer in Adelaide to prove intent; the fact that Shaun had gone to a family lawyer for the property transfer to his son, supported Mary's assertion that Shaun transferred the property after a disagreement with her in 2013, just to deny her its value. In producing the cheque out of context Dudley, in effect, used smoke and mirrors to pull a rabbit out of a hat.

Bingo! Dudley was successful in selling the registrar an apparently sledge-hammer argument. The registrar determined the financial settlement should be, wait for it, between 70-75 percent in Mary's favour. It settled at 72.5 percent, giving Mary all and more than she had expected ($361K), leaving Shaun with $65K (13 percent of his life's savings), after his legal debts were met.

While Mary hit the jackpot, Shaun hit a brick wall. Shaun's desperate disagreement with the decision was ignored. He told the registrar that the real reason for the property transfer to his son was for medical and welfare reasons and that these were documented. It was not done to deny Mary its value. Also, that the property could not have been quickly transferred after an alleged argument with Mary in 2013, because the process had commenced years before, on which documentary evidence was available. Shaun's arguments fell on deaf ears. Many material matters had dropped off the radar for the registrar.

Critical matters fell into obscurity the moment the registrar chose to believe Mary than Shaun. Her firm stance gave Shaun a binary choice: accept or appeal. She asked no questions. She gave no reason for her decision nor did she refer to relevant mitigating and contrary factors on file that were being implicitly discounted or rejected. The registrar coolly foreclosed on the many burning material issues which we shall go on to later present. The registrar's firmness obscured in shadow the resultant plight of an innocent third party, namely disabled Matthew.

The metaphorical fat lady sang 'Kumbaya.' There was a standing ovation accompanied by jubilant cheers from one side of the court theatre, even as the registrar brought down the final curtain in time for lunch. At long last the memorably dramatic life event concluded.

9.5 The Aftermath

What was a stunning victory for Mary was a body blow for Shaun. There were triumphal handshakes and joyous kisses in Mary's camp. Hands down victory was delivered to Mary in a crushing final act that enriched Mary as never before. Amazingly, she was given even more than she wanted, thereby putting icing on the cake. A now well-heeled Mary triumphantly swaggered out of the courtroom regarding the money as her legitimate entitlement. Her stubborn stance had been fully vindicated by the Family Court, no less.

In marked contrast, the settlement caught Shaun's lawyer Gianna unprepared and flabbergasted a hapless Shaun. It was a moment of truth; they were stunned into accepting a baffling outcome with weary resignation. Hobbled by his circumstances, Shaun was in no position to put up a fight to ward off the overwhelming blow. While both parties were at that moment put out of their misery of being under the dark shadow of a court case, a shell-shocked Shaun staggered away in dazed despair feeling like death warmed over. He realised he was condemned to be forever on the rack.

Let us pause to reflect on the several dimensions of what happened. Getting 13 percent of the asset pool after meeting legal costs meant that most of Shaun's superannuation life savings were gone, and he was condemned to always be a renter. He could never buy himself a retirement apartment that would have cost around $200K, and he was unable to undertake his legal duty to maintain his disabled son's trust property, that would require at least an additional $90K if son Matthew was to live to 80 years of age. That property sacrificed for love had suddenly become a millstone for Shaun. He was forever condemned to live well below his accustomed standard of living, while Mary was able to exceed the high standard of living that Shaun had elevated her to. Shaun's many years of planning for a reasonable retirement and peaceful death collapsed in a tragic heap. Two lives were devastated by the registrar's momentous determination that had given Mary everything but the kitchen sink. It was an evil moment of denouement for Shaun that forever cast a pall over his life and ability to care for his son.

Although it may at first glance seem justified, there is a lot more to the registrar's determination than meets the eye. Presented in the following chapter is the slew of burning issues that the registrar presumably duly considered in reaching her momentous determination, but seemingly largely discounted or disregarded. Since those numerous matters made Shaun dissatisfied with the decision, does it mean he should have rejected the registrar's so-called recommendation and gone on to a court trial?

9.6 Trial Hazards

The decision to proceed to a court trial is rarely an occasion for joyous tap dancing. Generally, court cases take 2-3 years, thereby adding to the trying ponderous pace of several months to the pre-trial stage – and typically costing at least a further $50K to boot. Till such time litigants' lives will be on hold. Placing lives in painful cold storage guarantees nothing because a favourable court trial outcome is a long way from being assured.

Going on to a court trial can often be a fool's errand; trials are fraught with uncertainty for litigants. After what for most frazzled litigants is an agonising wait, the court trial can be a huge gamble featuring wild cards from the litigants' standpoint. Litigants, like high rollers, face high penalties for errors when taking elevated risks based on mistaken expectations. Proceeding to trial will require subscription to a heroic assumption about functionality in the judicial system, as well as the brawny guts to discount the 'known unknowns' that plague it.

Can court trials be confidently described as a riot of justice? Individual solutions are crafted for different cases. Emotion-driven and highly variable family separation cases are by their very nature a long way from being open-and-shut. Evidence can get lost in the shuffle. Litigants may worry about the possibility that cases might come apart at the seams because of time pressure and human foibles.

Is there perfect justice that guarantees ironclad outcomes? The further question arises whether every overworked judge would inevitably be an exemplar of judicial wisdom each and every time. What is the guarantee that due to time pressure, case complexity, and moral strain, some judges sometimes will *never* lack academic rigour, forget issues, promise to return to something but never do and, moreover, find it devilishly hard to understand the tangled idiosyncrasies of personality disorders?

Dilemmas abound. For example, the judge might brush off what a wife regards as major faults in her husband, such as his failure to change nappies. Because of communication gaps, what is an open book to aggrieved litigants may be a closed book to the judge from the litigants' viewpoint. Judges are human beings and can have different points of view on the same matter. Just two of many examples were the disagreements with their colleagues by Justice

Kay and Justice Nygh on separate occasions as reported in *Quarterly Essay* (Hirst 2005 pp18-19).

Do women have an inside track? Although judges are usually gender neutral, litigants not sharing in that confidence may question whether or not, in the words of Edmund Burke (1729-1797), they had "the cold neutrality of an impartial judge." To state an obvious legal principle: the absence of neutrality automatically renders the written law irrelevant and judgements arbitrary.

These realities highlight lurking risks for litigants. Although the wheels of justice are known to grind slowly, do they really grind exceeding small (to paraphrase Henry Longfellow, 1807-1882)? Lawyers with a total of 80 years of experience among them in the Family Court system have made allegations with regard to all the aforementioned matters. It has also been alleged by those lawyers that in all that time they could count on the fingers of one hand the judicial decisions that lived up to litigant expectations. That implies, from the litigant standpoint, victory would be a fine thing if it happens because a favourable result is a surprise.

"Prediction is difficult, especially about the future," as Neil Bohr (1885-1962) famously observed. Although there is a desperate need to know one's chances at a trial, predictability is alarmingly scanty – and the expected outcome can seem a toss-up to potential litigants. Fathoming with reasonable certainty which way the cat will jump requires the services of a crystal ball in the circumstances. Consequently, an anticipated result for a particular litigant will need to be based more on hope than expectation.

9.7 Conciliation Ambiguity

In light of the above, the registrar's offer to Shaun was insidiously fraught. For Shaun, the registrar's determination of 72.5/27.5 (68/13 after costs) in favour of Mary effectively meant: 'your money or your life.'

Nay was not an option within reason. Refusing to accept the registrar's so-called recommendation would have condemned the case to a daunting court trial. That would have required at least two more years in limbo for Shaun now aged 77 years and ailing, on top of the nightmarish 16 months already experienced that had brought him to death's door. Furthermore, going to trial would have pushed up costs by more than $50K in addition to his already frightful legal bill of $65K.

The process was flummoxing for Shaun. The practical reality was that the registrar's 'recommendation' was in effect a verdict – it was a ruling that had *fait accompli* written all over it. She called the shots because Shaun's age, financial condition, and health gave rise to a compulsion of circumstances. Given Shaun's mental, physical, and financial fatigue at the time, the registrar's so-called recommendation really meant that Shaun should settle or risk death – fatigue compelling submission to injustice as he subjectively saw it.

The registrar's determination could only be rejected at peril. Nowhere is it recorded that the case resolved under duress. Duress is an eminently valid consideration because it has respectable legal standing. Since there is every indication that Shaun succumbed to pressure, did the compulsion of Shaun's circumstances warrant the legal status of duress?

As shown, there are more questions than answers. The open questions demanding answers are associated with issues fundamental to the delivery of justice in the Family Court system. They are broken down into their constituent parts for deeper analysis in the following narrative.

***

Chapter 10

QUALIFYING INFORMATION: BURNING ISSUES

10.1 Open Questions

An injurious falsehood emerged victorious. The registrar discounted or disregarded the information on file to believe the person with questionable testimony and disbelieve the person whose testimony had never been questioned. That Mary and lawyer Dudley had previously lied was actually recorded on file, and that was besides the dismissal of Mary's police testimony in the Local Court case. Yet their word was given greater weight than was Shaun's by the registrar. But that was the least of it.

Several issues stand out a mile. Looking wider and deeper detects a number of issues of fact and law having material status and crying out for consideration. Identified below are crucial matters that the registrar presumably duly considered in her determination, but which she nevertheless seems to have discounted or disregarded, perhaps with good reason, albeit undisclosed.

The perspective next adopted is wide and inclusive. In the following narrative, a broad social perspective subsumes a narrow legal angle for presenting a bigger picture from a lay standpoint. The qualifying material issues are comprehensive and are examined next under the three headings: Matters of Fact; Matters of Family Law; and Matters of Social Security Law. Take each in turn.

10.2 Matters of Fact

A cheque was regarded as the smoking gun. The registrar's decision in Mary's favour mainly depended on the evidence of a cheque payment for the property transfer having been made to a family lawyer by Shaun. This supported Mary's allegation that the property transfer to his disabled son under Commonwealth law was done to deny her its value following a family dispute. No mention was made of the secret transfers by Mary of her and Shaun's assets to *her* son that denied Shaun *their* value. But that digresses, so hold that thought for now until more is later stated on that important point of law in relation to section 79(4) of the Family Law Act.

That single factor of the cheque seemingly outweighed everything else. The reason that Shaun went to the family lawyer Diana for the property transfer was because he lived in a different city and she had been recommended by a mutual friend. Diana took on the task of setting up the trust for Matthew despite it being outside her field, rather than telling him to go elsewhere. Yet a cheque evidencing payment to lawyer Diana was a crucial, if not the sole, basis for the registrar's 'recommendation,' that wreaked havoc on Shaun.

A lie was believed. Mary's assertion that Shaun went to see the family lawyer Diana after an argument in 2013 (one that Shaun could not remember) and transferred the property to deny her its value was contradicted by other direct evidence on two counts. One count was the property transfer process commenced over one year before the alleged argument that supposedly triggered it. The second count was that Mary could not have been denied the value of a property that had no value to Shaun.

Regarding the first count, dates did not match. The process of transferring the property had commenced at least one year previous to the supposed argument with Mary that allegedly precipitated it. That was when Shaun wrote to the tax department seeking a confirmatory ruling that the transfer of the property (that was to be held in trust for his son under Centrelink aegis pursuant to the Social Security Act 1991) would be exempt from capital gains tax. That he did because, as his investment property, its transfer would usually have attracted such a tax. There was evidence of the correspondence confirming the exemption from tax that well predated the time of the alleged argument that was claimed by Mary to have precipitated the transfer of the property to Matthew.

Was the motivation for the property transfer 'beyond reasonable doubt'? What prompted Shaun to attempt to transfer the property to his son was a resurgence of his heart condition combined with information from Matthew's psychiatrist that accommodation security was crucial to Matthew. Matthew's apartment served as a therapeutic hideaway – a sanctuary which kept him off the streets where he had previously been. That psychiatrist's position was later confirmed by certificatory letters from the mental health service as well as by Centrelink. It was no ordinary transfer for a normal purpose, but was it treated like it was?

Do the preceding issues put a noteworthy dent in the winning argument? The evidence gives some reason to question Mary's claim that Shaun's intent to transfer the property was to deny Mary its value. Therefore, there is some reason to believe the transfer was because of love and caring for his son, not to deny Mary its value. This point, put to the registrar by Shaun, was expressly rejected by her. For the registrar, it seems there was no reasonable doubt to Mary's argument despite the inconsistent documentary evidence on file (to be shortly addressed in more detail).

Regarding the second count, there were no sale proceeds. The other counterargument rests on whether Mary could have been denied the value of a property that had no value to Shaun. The registrar's determination conferred a benefit from the property on Mary even though Shaun did not, and could not, get any benefit from the property. It was transferred to the government for free (without any sales proceeds) under Commonwealth legislation. Its value is locked away till the trust is dissolved upon son Matthew's death or when the trust becomes financially nonviable. The property to Shaun was a liability, not an asset. More on that later.

The matter of relative legal costs was never raised. Registrars are expected to look at relative legal costs, especially considering that Mary had imposed significant legal costs of $32K on Shaun from arguably unwarranted court cases, one to eject her and the other for the dismissed restraining order. At that time Mary was on legal aid and her total legal bill was roughly a third of Shaun's. Shaun's total cost of about $65K was nearly half of the settlement offer put forward by the registrar. After meeting legal costs Shaun's share of the settlement was 13 percent of the asset pool ($65K), while Mary's share was 68 percent ($340K).

10.3 Matters of Family Law

Many open questions of a legal nature jump out. In addition to the foregoing factual matters, there is no information on why several factors, firmly based in the Family Law, were discounted or disregarded by the registrar in her determination. Because of their profound legal nature, they are presented here more as questions posed than answers provided.

Relative contributions are a crucial consideration. Under section 79(4) of the Family Law Act contributions can be non-financial and financial. The party making the larger contribution is entitled to the larger settlement, provided adequate provision is made for the reasonable living of both parties. The idea being the settlement must be just and equitable. 'Just' refers to fairness, all factors considered; 'equitable' refers to even-handedness.

Legal orthodoxy assumes a non-monetary contribution by the partner. At the heart of the Family Law is the sacrosanct 'no-fault' principle that is fundamental to all aspects of it. In the property settlement, in terms of the 'no-fault' principle, the assets have to be divided according to contributions the parties have made to its acquisition and enhancement. In the case of the family home, although it was purchased solely from Shaun's earnings (his superannuation), Mary is deemed to have contributed to the property in non-financial terms, usually by virtue of a homemaker role. The partner is assumed to have cooked the food and kept the place tidy, although that may have rarely or never happened. Usually the homemaker role is at least partly justified by the fact that wives invest their labour and time in bringing up children. Of course, there were no children involved in this case, except for Shaun's partly dependant son Matthew who lived elsewhere. Mary had made no contribution to the acquisition of the family home or to its financial maintenance (such as for strata fees, rates, refurbishment and repairs), but had instead milked the relationship. For unknown reasons, these factors were not considered as diminishing Mary's contribution to the marriage in the final assessment.

Shaun made a standard 50/50 offer to expedite settlement. Specifically, Shaun's settlement offer was not altered to reflect the peculiar circumstances of this particular case, so as not to complicate matters. Mary did not have the lifestyle of a typical housewife; many aspects of Mary's lifestyle were alien to the usual 'homemaker' yardstick. Shaun had lavished on Mary over 132 overseas trips at a cost of over $400K; their life together on prolonged overseas travel for up to six months of the year, did not involve homemaking. And there was minimal homemaking in the high-end lifestyle while in Australia, as it featured regular restaurant meals. In contrast, Mary's contribution was a cavernous negative. However, Shaun's initial offer of 50/50 implied acceptance of the standard application of the Family Law and ignored his extraordinary contribution to the marriage and Mary's financial milking. Despite its conformity to orthodoxy, that offer was, of course, summarily rejected because of Mary's fixation on getting 70 percent of the total asset pool.

The other property was a different matter. Disabled son Matthew's property (now owned by the government and held in a Special Disability Trust), was the central bone of contention and raised legal issues of an unusual type. Shaun had purchased it out of funds brought into the relationship (nil contribution by Mary), and Mary had not contributed to its enhancement as is assumed to happen in regard to the family home under the 'no-fault' principle (no 'homemaker' role there). On the contrary, instead of contributing to that property, Mary's household had benefited from its net rental income for 16 years. So the previously mentioned point, regarding non-financial contribution through 'homemaking' applicable to the family home, clearly did not apply to the property transferred by Shaun to his son Matthew.

Bur property transfers are of key relevance to settlement. What applied to Shaun's son's property was the requirement in the Family Law that all property transfers during the course of the marriage should be taken into account. That is particularly so if the property was transferred to deny the partner its value.

But several other Family Law provisions come into play that may possibly dilute, if not override, the validity of the foregoing provision.

For a start, critical mitigating factors are that the property to disabled son Matthew was transferred gratis (there were no sales proceeds), was done for a certified medical purpose, was authorised under Commonwealth law, and could not be sold. It was owned by the government under Commonwealth legislation. This alleviating legal dimension is crucial and will be returned to later in relation to the Social Security Act 1991.

Moreover, were the property transfers to their respective offspring by the parties given equal or unequal weight in the registrar's determination? It is not known whether or not her treatment of this matter meets the 'just and equitable' criterion.

Since Shaun's transfer of his property to the government on behalf of his son was relevant to the registrar's decision on settlement, was Mary's transfer of the sales proceeds of her property to her children, as recorded with Centrelink, taken into consideration but discounted? Also, was Mary's secret transfer of over $304K of household and pension monies to support her son Ashley for 20 years of relevance to the registrar's decision? Was there no intent on Mary's part to deny Shaun the value of her assets? If Shaun's transfer of an apartment for a medical purpose to his disabled son under Commonwealth law was relevant to settlement, did that make Mary's transfers to her able-bodied son under dubious circumstances also relevant? No cancelling-out effect there?

The inputs to the relationship by the parties are a vital aspect under The Family Law Act, as earlier stated. Accordingly, the registrar presumably factored into her determination Shaun's lavish contribution on the one hand, and Mary's negative contribution on the other. The evidence recorded Shaun was more than a good provider, having given Mary a five-star life style. Shaun had spent $400 on her travel, $72K on medical costs, and done things for her that were over and above normal with the purchase of an expensive hairpiece, regular restaurant meals, money on her grandchildren, *inter alia*. In stark contrast, Mary had surreptitiously withheld her two overseas pensions from Shaun and secretly transferred her Centrelink pension and house proceeds to the children from her previous marriage. It is a mystery as to what extent the colossal disparity in relative contributions to the marriage by the parties mattered in the registrar's determination.

The Family Court places heavy emphasis on the welfare of children. The Court takes the view that in separation the best interest of the child is paramount. A particular concern is how to ensure that the parent can best assist the child as a responsible parent. Court decisions taken should enable parents to attend to their child's developmental needs and promote their child's best interest.

But that is only when the parties to the relationship have children together. Surprisingly, this concern does not seem to extend to a disabled child from a former marriage for whom one party has legally defined responsibility. Shaun's responsibility to his disabled son's property is expressly laid down in his Trust Deed as is required by the Commonwealth Social Security Act 1991. Did the registrar discount or reject Shaun's responsibility to his son under Commonwealth law?

Section 75.2 of the Family Law Act is no dead letter. Under that section of the Family Law, the registrar is obliged to consider the future requirements of the parties to the marriage by considering age, health, financial resources and the ability to earn. Why was the loss to Shaun of 87 percent of his superannuation retirement savings acceptable to the registrar, considering the indisputable fact that the loss was worryingly durable due to his inability to work on account of age and health?

The registrar is even required to ensure a standard of living that in all circumstances is reasonable. That implies the parties should have a standard of living they were accustomed to. With Shaun being left with 13 percent of his total life's savings after his legal costs were met, the registrar decision boosted Mary's already elevated standard of living while causing Shaun's to take a nosedive to deny him his accustomed quality of life. Was it appropriate that Mary's standard of living should far exceed that of Shaun's, even forgetting Shaun's responsibility to maintain his son's property? Why did the registrar deem that it met the 'just and equitable' criterion?

Section 75 of the Family Law Act is blackletter law that protects the helpless. Expressly mentioned there is the responsibility of a party to support another person and the commitments necessary to provide for themselves or a child. Children are regarded as having a right to a safe and stable home – the very thing that the registrar's determination took away from Shaun's disabled son. It is most puzzling as to why the registrar used Commonwealth legislation (The Family Law Act 1975) to deny protection to an innocent third party deemed by the welfare agency Centrelink to qualify for such protection under other Commonwealth legislation (The Social Security Act 1991).

10.4 Matters of Social Security Law

The registrar's determination raises deeper questions still.

Was the imputation of value to a non-tradable asset valid? The registrar took the position that the Mary should be compensated for the transfer of the property to Shaun's son Matthew even though she had contributed nothing towards it, because it was done to deny her its value. But there was no value; the property was transferred for free, at zero sales price, and for a special purpose under Commonwealth legislation. The Commonwealth government got a dual benefit from the transfer: it no longer needed to provide for Matthew's accommodation on account of his disability at any time in the future; and it no longer needed to pay the Centrelink rental allowance. Having to compensate Mary was a double-whammy for Shaun – the property transfer engendered a benefit to society and was now made to also benefit Mary, both benefits given at Shaun's expense.

Was the property treated as an asset when it was really a liability? Having been transferred under Centrelink aegis to the Public Trustee without consideration, the apartment occupied by Shaun's son was now owned by the government and was no longer an asset for Shaun. He could not sell it. It was, in fact, a liability because, although its rental income ceased, it had still to be maintained at the cost of $3000/year for strata, rates repairs, etc., by Shaun, and for the rest of the occupant's life (estimated to be $90K till age 80). The registrar's determination took away the money needed for that purpose, and gave it to Mary under conditions where it was inessential for her living; it was bonus by $111K in excess of the 50/50 offer already on the table. The registrar by her determination pursuant to the Family Law Act 1975 denied Shaun the ability to undertake his legal obligation under the Social Security Act 1991 to maintain his son Mathew's property for the rest of Matthew's life.

The property transfer was under Commonwealth Law. Even if, as the registrar seemingly believed, the property was transferred to deny Mary its value, it was transferred for the purpose of giving accommodation security to a person whom Centrelink had determined, under the Social Security Act 1991, was disabled enough to qualify for the transfer. Moreover, there was a certificate issued by the mental health agency attesting to the fact that accommodation security was essential for the disabled person's health and welfare, as well as a confirmatory letter from Centrelink to Shaun on the same matter. That means, Shaun was exercising a right created under the Social Security Act 1991. The registrar effectively used the Family Law Act 1975 to rightly or wrongly punish Shaun for exercising a right granted to him under the Social Security Act 1991.

Which law is superior: The Family Law Act 1975 or the Social Security Act 1991? As the property was transferred under the Commonwealth Social Security Act 1991, was the registrar saying the Family Law Act 1975 automatically overrode citizens' rights conferred on them by the Social Security Act 1991? What factors shaped the registrar's fateful determination on this far-reaching legal point?

What is more, and crucially, should Shaun have refrained from taking advantage of the protective rights for his son under the Social Security Act 1991 because of Mary's objections? The registrar's determination seems to imply so. The registrar's decision meant that Mary's rights overrode Shaun's rights; what the registrar did was to determine that Mary had the right to prevent Shaun from exercising his rights granted under the Social Security Act 1991 to protect his son. Because Shaun did so against Mary's wishes, he now needed to compensate her for transferring the property even though she had contributed nothing towards it, and did not really need the money for her future living.

Was the situation inherently unequal? Mary was reaping benefits from a trust that provided no corresponding benefit to Shaun. That effectively meant that Shaun's legal obligations to his disabled son under Commonwealth legislation had become a rod for his own back.

10.5 Registrar Notes

The office of registrar is a position of public trust – implying that the duties must be performed in good faith without abuse or violation. A diligent registrar can be expected to have sifted salient points out of the documents on file before the start of the Conciliation Conference. Asking probing questions, seeking to understand matters better, would also have helped. The following crucial points can be expected to have featured in the notes of a competent registrar:

- The determination at the Conciliation Conference was effectively final. There were time compulsions on account of the age and health of the parties. Appeal was impractical.

- There were conflicting pieces of Commonwealth legislation in play. That raises a red flag alerting judicial caution. It was at least questionable that Mary's objections could prevent Shaun from exercising a right to protect his son conferred on him by the Social Security Act that, moreover, came with a legal responsibility recognised under section 75 of the Family Law Act.

- Mary's demand was unusual. Giving Mary her demand for settlement at 70/30 would leave Shaun with 13 percent of his life savings after his legal costs were met. Half his legal costs can be attributed to Mary's unwarranted and malicious actions. Relative legal costs of the parties qualified to be factored in.

- The contribution of each party to the relationship was lopsided. Shaun had lavished money for medical, travel, and living expenses on Mary whereas Mary had milked the relationship. Mary's financial contribution was purposefully withheld from Shaun, while her non-financial contribution was lower than usual because of their unusual lifestyle.

- The property transfer process to Shaun's disabled son was protracted. The lengthy process exceeding a period of three years could not have been precipitated by an argument in the middle of it as alleged by Mary.

- The property transfer was no ordinary transfer. The property was not just a home but a therapeutic sanctuary for the mentally disabled. It was done for the certified medical purpose of guaranteeing long-term accommodation security pursuant to Commonwealth law and under Centrelink and psychiatric supervision. It was recommended by the mental health service and was to be under its ongoing supervision.

- The property transfer could not deny value to Mary since it was of no value to Shaun. Mary had contributed nothing to its purchase or maintenance, but had yet benefitted from its rent for 16 years. The property was given to the government, there were no sale proceeds and it could not be sold. Mary should not be able to get value from a property that had no value to Shaun as stipulated in the Trust Deed under Commonwealth law.

- There were negating effects. Even if the property transfer by Shaun to the government showed intent to deny Mary its value (ignoring reasonable doubt regarding that argument), Mary's transfer of household monies and house sale proceeds to her offspring would have a negating effect on Shaun's transfer.

- Shaun had responsibility from legal dependency under section 75 of the Family Law Act. The Trust Deed required that the trust property be maintained by Shaun out of his funds for the rest of the occupant's life and that it be sold should maintenance become nonviable. So giving to Mary the superannuation savings of Shaun that had been set aside for the purpose implied future homelessness for the disabled third party. Shaun's legal responsibility under

Commonwealth law for the welfare of his partially dependant son was a crucial consideration.

- The settlement outcome was unequal. The settlement gave Mary a future lifestyle greater than that to which she was accustomed and took away 87 percent of Shaun's life savings after his costs were met, causing his lifestyle to sink well below that to which he was accustomed.

The registrar's determination, effectively a judicial ruling, was riddled with unknowns. Open questions haunt the conciliation outcome from a social justice standpoint. That refers to a standpoint where there is fair and just relation between the individual standpoint and the social standpoint.

The imperatives of social justice prompt three burning questions. Firstly, it is not known why the registrar, in giving consideration to the foregoing listing of points, chose to discount or disregard them. After all, the Family Law Act defines the fabric that must fashion the settlement. Therefore, discounting or disregarding information material to it seems worthy of an explanation. Secondly, it is not known whether or not the reasoning behind the registrar's determination would stand up to critical examination, had the case proceeded to trial. Thirdly, it is not known whether the registrar was required by 'no-fault' convention to follow a preordained standard script.

The last point needs elaboration. It raises the question of whether the registrar's determination was based on a narrow stereotypical template for a mechanical solution that was standard practice in the casual 'no-fault' conciliation situation, despite the case being distinctive on account of its unusual complexity. If an ordinary solution had been applied to this extraordinary case, it would have, by definition, excluded consideration of vital issues of a material nature integral to the peculiarities of the case, much of which were documented.

In the wake of the registrar's unflinching approach, burning questions surface on the matter of social justice at both the individual level and the social level. These are dissected for deeper examination in the post-mortem that follows.

***

Chapter 11
AUTOPSIC EVALUATION: DIRE FINDINGS

11.1 Thorny Issues

The preceding far-ranging issues frame the overarching nature of the case. The host of issues highlighted take the form of crucial questions on matters of fact and matters of law. The thorny legal questions raised require answers from judges who qualify as pantheons of judicial wisdom, since from a lay perspective they seemingly aggregate to a veritable gorse bush.

This was not a run-of-the-mill kind of case. Judging by the judicial depth and breadth of the aspects spotlighted in the preceding analysis, they unmistakably demand a high level of worldly wisdom from thinking outside the box. There were several matters of both a straightforward and challenging nature that qualified to be factored into the registrar's calculus in making her monetary determination. It cannot be known whether or not the registrar's determination was anything more than an offhand application of an inelegant rule-of-thumb that is standard practice in 'no-fault' conciliation situations – and is not expected to have much, if anything, to do with material facts of the case.

Whither justice? The paramount question is not who won, but whether justice was served. Justice is much more than money sought by mercenary individuals like Mary, who see justice through the prism of money – a perspective where money is justice and justice is money. While the matter of who won is at the level of the individual person, justice is necessarily societal. That means the Roman personification of justice, the allegorical goddess Justitia, would be indifferent as to who wins, but only when, contrary to the picture depicted on the cover of this book, she is blindfolded and holding evenly balanced scales.

Examined next are how the wheel of justice turned, what imperatives drove it, and what sort of trail was left in its wake. That uncovers winners and losers at the individual level, and the traits and quirks of institutions at the social level. The following matters are looked at through the narrow perceptual lens of the persons involved on the one hand, and from the panoramic standpoint of society on the other.

11.2 The Personal Angle

For Mary, justice was delivered at the self-interested personal level. It was a slam dunk for lawyer Dudley and a triumph for client Mary. The golden calf of victory, more of mammon than of angels, was handed to Mary on a platter by the registrar. Mary's intransigence had masked a winning formula. Her large settlement was a bonanza that vindicated all the deviousness in her unremitting quest designed to get just that.

It was an outstanding piece of strategy. Spurred by avarice, Mary's targeting of Shaun's dependent mentally disabled son's apartment in the final settlement was a merciless masterstroke that made her dream of riches come true and imposed painful permanent punishment on her two targeted enemies. Mary and lawyer Dudley had not only cannily ambushed Shaun and his lawyer Gianna, but also cleverly caused the registrar to make a reality of their wishes. A dual victory for Mary was a double whammy for Shaun.

For Shaun, the outcome was a train wreck. From his viewpoint, justice rang hollow, particularly because it had a social dimension to it on account of his legal responsibility to his mentally disabled son. To his knowledgeable mind, apart from the pain of ingratitude from Mary, the registrar's decision was a bolt from the blue that took away his ability to care for his son and most of his superannuation life savings. As a truthful person, it was hard for him to swallow the registrar's disbelieving of his objections, which were in any case supported by documentary evidence. That was additional to the bad memory of the creative range of process abuses by Mary and her lawyers leading up to the disastrous culmination, that had already made justice look like something the cat brought in.

Was Shaun's shaken confidence in the justice system justified? That cannot be known since the registrar's decision was not accompanied by any reasoning, and Shaun's objections to her decision were rejected without explanation. He was tormented by the mystery as to why none of the many matters raised in section 10.5 came to his rescue. The absence of the need for any sort of explanation on even one of the many points raised makes the conciliation decision-making process lax by definition. At the risk of tautology, the absence of reasons for disregarding or discounting crucially relevant information made the registrar's decision inexplicable – that is, beyond comprehension. Given the brittle informality that underpinned the process, booting high stakes issues to low formality conciliation gave Shaun reason to question whether the system had thrown up a stunningly prejudicial outcome that denied him and his son their substantive rights.

The great promise of 'no-fault' became a grave peril for Shaun. Shaun was made to pay a hefty price for showing love and caring for his son. He was further punished by being made to pay for someone else's bad behaviour, namely pay for Mary's pile of faults that the 'no-fault' basis had ironically facilitated, if not encouraged. It galled him that Mary, who claimed before the court to be a charity-giving Christian and whom he knew to be a regular churchgoer, would so avidly hanker after gains from the mammon of unrighteousness. From Shaun's subjective angle, the profusion of faults that injured him made 'no-fault' a travesty and the settlement at conciliation as antithetic to fairness as evil is to love.

'No-fault' permissiveness enabled Shaun's lawyer Gianna to be outmanoeuvred. She got the short end of the stick due to opposition Dudley's dirty trick. Dudley's late, last-minute, filing, a sleazy unpunctuality emblematically tolerated without objection by the 'no-fault' Family Court process, did not give her the time and the opportunity to ponder the unpredicted. She was unable to thoroughly reflect on the matter and come up with the aforementioned counter arguments to the startling red herring let loose by Mary's lawyer.

Yet Gianna had failed to warn Shaun of the possible outcome. Her putting a brave face on things cannot mask the fact that she was unable to see what was coming and prepare for the possibility. The question arises whether the inbuilt pressure for a speedy resolution in conciliation experienced in this case, was an institutionalised pressure for injustice. If so there would be agonising dissonance between quick fixes and just outcomes.

11.3 The Social Angle

Getting a handle on the basics will expose root causes. That requires stepping back to consider the bigger picture from the standpoint of society, by eliciting a *general* message from this *particular* case. What we see goes to the heart of the Family Court's raison d'être, namely its singular and revered 'no-fault' basis.

As rigour erodes, justice recedes. The laudable 'no-fault' basis designed for easy justice can foster a quick-fix disposition that hampers justice. Procedural rigour is the wellspring of justice. If a miscarriage of justice does occur, it would be enabled by the slack and informal judicial processes associated with 'no-fault' that can be lackadaisical to a fault. Since taking all material facts into consideration is the *sine qua non* for valid justice, it is not rocket science to realise that ignoring material facts would truncate perspectives and give rise to determinations studded with deviancy – implying departures from justice. It beggars belief that cutting corners for quick fixes within the casual judicial channel will not make injustice an eminently logical effluent. If justice were indeed absent, what would then prevail are the trappings of a legal system sans a justice system.

There is a sobering gap between theory and practice. For the majority of disputants the reality is that, while the registrars' recommendation could be turned down in theory, the risks are too high in practice. While registrars do not hold a pistol to anyone's head, their technically euphemistic 'recommendation' can have much more than a tinge of diktat to it. The question arises whether generally the trappings of conciliation provide window dressing for perpetrating the hoax that the outcomes result from voluntary agreements between the parties, when they are in reality the result of judicial rulings by registrars.

The facts back the argument. The statistics reveal that over 90 percent of cases resolve before the trial stage. The wearied, when cornered, can cede their discretion out of resignation. Physical and financial exhaustion, coupled with anxiety due to the touch-and-go dark cloud of uncertainty at the trial stage, likely explains much of the high rate of resolution at the earlier stage. Although that is so irrespective of age and state of health of disputants, the conditions of age and health assume high relevance to registrar determinations when they signify duress.

The office of registrar is one of public trust. Since the fate of innocents is in the trust of registrars, it goes without saying that it is vital registrars have knowledge and perspective from properly studying the file. The resultant professional soundness is crucial to compensate for the informality inherent in the 'no-fault' process. Only when so equipped will registrars have the professional capability to stare overbearing and crafty lawyers full in the face. Competent and neutral registrars are therefore an essential bulwark against lawyers who use 'no-fault' permissiveness to run rings around them by: making a drama of issues; introducing red herrings to distract them from real issues; using bluster to play who dares wins; or in other unethical ways pulling the wool over registrars' eyes.

For Family Court fans, why spoil the fantasy with the facts? On the face of it, the mission of the Family Court is fulfilled by the pragmatism of a quick 'no-fault' fix at the conciliation stage. The avoidance of a court trial gives a favourable signal to those blinded by ostrichism and persisting against odds with faith in the grand 'no-fault' dream. They are able to peddle the illusion that all is fair and square and that resolution at conciliation proves the conciliation process was actually working. That sanguine belief explains the convenient catechism of those ignoring the cloven hoof of unjustness. A blinkered view that misses the beguiling insidiousness of a blundering conciliation outcome would happily mistake geese for swans. Such a view is likely to be oblivious of nervous wrecks sapped of motivation and lacking the verve to up the ante by rejecting registrars' unjust determinations.

Statistics by themselves are silent. To be soothed by the statistical evidence that over 90 percent of cases resolve at the pre-trial stage eschews Mark Twain's hierarchy of notoriety of there being lies, damned lies, and statistics. That gives a big tick for statistics and a sense of accomplishment for vested interests. The tragic consequence of a casual and opaque decision process, in a situation where registrars are not up to speed, would then give rise to the following absurdity: while the statistics of measuring the Family Court's success bumps up a notch (and registrars get a feather in their cap), that could well have been achieved at the cost of human carnage. If so, it makes a daydream of the belief that pre-trial resolution inevitably manifests successful justice; what seem solutions might in fact be bungles.

Only scientific research will enable policymakers to avoid a bum steer. Knowing the score will reveal the extent to which this case is typical – that is, the extent to which the several reported process failures throughout the investigated case are illustrative examples having general relevance. That obviously must include the highlight of whether the case in point is representative of what generally happens at the critical make-or-break pre-trial decision-making stage. It is important to know if it is the exception or the rule because, in the words of Barack Obama, although "our stories are singular, our destiny is shared." Hence the research problem to be diagnosed is simply this: are the high percentage of cases that do not go to trial a barometer of system malfunction, rather than evidence of successful justice? That immediately raises the challenging question of what proportion of cases delivering full-blown justice would qualify the Family Court for a cheery thumbs-up 'good performance' rating.

Is power without responsibility an inherent feature of the Conciliation Conference? The failure to ask questions or give reasons for decisions at the conciliation stage introduces casualness into the process that is jarringly at odds with responsible conduct. That is particularly so when documented information material to the case in hand is being disregarded or discounted. Although a tightly reasoned argument might be too much to expect, a stunning void from deafening silence can make today's resolution at conciliation tomorrow's skeleton in the Family Court cupboard.

Opaqueness obscures the finger of responsibility. More specifically, the absence of explanation can deny accountability to the court of public opinion when it shrouds mistreatment of the innocent by registrars. Since most cases are resolved at the pre-trial stage, registrars are the soft underbelly of the entire Family Court system. When informality restricts perspective, registrars can insidiously degrade the legal mainstay of 'no-fault' for Potemkin justice. This view finds support in John Hirst's statement on 'no-fault' in *Quarterly Essay*: "The Family Court is a monstrosity, a court of law that cannot by its no-fault charter be a court of justice" (Hirst 2005, p74). What transpires then is a semblance of justice; justice in form but not substance. That could make 'no-fault' a euphemism for unjust pragmatism – specifically, it could make 'no-fault' the cause of stereotypical off-hand rule-of-thumb determinations removed from material facts. If there is no fair shake from an even break, would not what is hailed as success really be scandal?

An affirmative answer only begs the question. The deeper question is whether, beneath the facade of pre-trial settlements for reassuring public appeasement, there is underlying institutional atrophy in the Family Court system; whether an insidious cancer thrives, not necessarily due to the law itself, but due to the manner of its implementation. In slipshod circumstances of institutional permissiveness, where there is no transparency or accountability for life-changing registrar determinations, and they, moreover, fly in the face of mitigating or contrary information material to the case in hand, could registrars be delivering a caricature of justice as a typical takeaway - making what is hailed as success to really be failure?

If so, it could it mean that dodgy justice is common and lurking. If that be the case, the following implication emerges: there would then be present a hidden weeping wound in the Family Court system. "When Family Court judges talk piously of the 'caring court' I wish they could hear the roar of pain their piety has caused" (Hirst, p6). If the grand dream of 'no-fault' utopia has generally degenerated into a rough-justice nightmare, it raises the worrying question of whether we have a justice system worthy of its name.

That sobering question implies a distressingly fatalistic view of the Family Court system. It explains an end result to this case that is ripe with symbolism. Nobody called Mary out on her audacious misdeeds enabled and encouraged by the judicial permissiveness inherent in the 'no-fault' Family Court system. With help from complicit lawyers, Mary managed to thumb her nose at legal and ethical propriety, play the system, and still emerge smelling of roses. Despite Mary's unscrupulous moves, or perhaps because of them, the Family Court's 'no-fault' blessings handed Mary the last laugh.

***

Chapter 12

CONCLUSION: LOST CAUSE?

12.1 Absent Nobility

The Family Court is a special type of court. It is a civil court, not a criminal court, built on the foundation of noble intent. It is differentiated from other courts by its professed caring mission based on 'no-fault' divorce. That makes sense as the disputants are usually not criminals, just ordinary people, your average Joe and Jill Bloggs, traumatised by failure in their relationship.

When in the process of separation, ordinary people find themselves in an extraordinary situation. The parties to the separation are in the process of experiencing a major life crisis. There is a death of sorts, since grief is part and parcel of relationship breakdown, with at least one partner needing to navigate turbulence. Their circumstances are typically unprecedented and scary. Family separation can be said to be the second most horrible thing that can happen to a human being, the first one being the death of a child to a parent. The lives of parties to a separation, when configured by a lengthy Family Court agenda, are condemned to simmer with tension. Consequently, suffering psychological pressure becomes a test of endurance for most.

When in that sorry state, strangers enter their lives and whisk them away into the realm of tortuous government. The control that disputants have over their lives will drain away as lawyers increasingly take over and use the undertow of the Family Law to invade their privacy and lay bare their lives. The unbridled public intrusion into previously private space enables delicate matters to be fair game for embarrassing disclosure. Abundant headaches for clients generate ample fees for lawyers. Ongoing contact with their lawyer and an unpleasant series of court appearances will entwine the lives of clients and lawyers for the purpose of muddling through a rolling series of crises.

So that puts family lawyers in a special place? What has just been stated may create an expectation that family lawyers in the thick of human unhappiness, when compared to criminal court lawyers, are a breed apart and a cut above in terms of kindness and compassion. Perhaps they would, in accordance with the Family Court's professed caring mission, show empathy and be committed to getting a fair shake for both parties. One would expect them to advise their emotion-driven clients on the rational and the reasonable for equitable outcomes, especially when there are knock-on effects that involve the welfare of innocent and helpless children.

There is not much hope of that, if the conduct of the majority of lawyers featured in the investigated case is anything to go by. The culprit lawyers had little inclination to be gripped by a sense of compassion or be activated by a sense of urgency. These traits were found to be outside the bounds of their professional calling. They ignored the niceties of ethical behaviour and thought nothing of broader issues of truth and justice. They were compulsively driven to win – and at any cost. Being fixated on winning for their client meant harming already suffering human beings was all in a day's work. It was of little concern that court processes were abused for undue advantage, obfuscation was tactical, the discovery process was weaponized, registrars misled with porous arguments, or that the mentally disabled were rendered homeless. They gave no quarter; ambition trumped propriety.

12.2 Falling Short

The Family Law Act 1975 was to be a game changer. The fanfare accompanying the introduction of the Family Law Act 1975 trumpeted it as a big deal that broke new ground for society. It was a hard-won victory for social reformers advocating the innovation. Betting the farm on 'no-fault' separation made sense when it promised to repel turmoil from bitter partners being at each other's throats. Caring and friendliness were to be the defining traits of the dedicated Family Court system. It was to facilitate a less angry and more respectful way of ending a relationship that *both* parties agreed was over.

The current reality is jarring when juxtaposed against that idealised hope. The several dispiriting factors haunting disputants caught up in the Family Court system are not hard to find for those bothering to look closely enough. The more insightful will see in the Family Court system a pathetic disease-ridden patient feigning normality. The scrutinized case illustratively brought to light the disorderly abnormalities afflicting that organism.

Faulty 'No-fault'

The golden calf of 'no-fault' has acquired a brassy finish. The civilised 'no-fault' basis has not turned out to be the promised panacea, as was amply illustrated by the case in point. The 'no-fault' basis ironically encourages fault and then conceals it.

Faults that are socially objectionable can be legally acceptable. There is divergence between what the average person in society may regard as faulty behaviour and what the Family Law Act regards as faulty behaviour – for an anomalous disconnect between the social and the legal. That means, paradoxically, the 'no-fault' basis can nurture and nourish anti-social faults of the sort that wife Mary in the examined case was shown to have engaged in. In effect Mary said: 'I have decided to leave you because I want to give more money to my children from my previous marriage than I have done already, and that includes the value of your disabled son's trust property; that your son's property would, as a result, be rendered financially nonviable and he homeless, is not my concern.' The case showed that husband Shaun was required to compensate wife Mary for providing for his disabled son from a previous marriage – provision legally required, moreover, under Commonwealth legislation. No fault there? No fault whatsoever, as implied in the Family Court's determination.

No reason is necessary to leave a relationship. Anyone can unilaterally decide to walk out on their partner at the drop of a hat. Either partner can leave against their partner's wishes, the law siding with the party violating the contract – implying that a marriage contract is unenforceable and susceptible to fraud.

The examined case shows up the 'no-fault' Family Law as capable of being omnipresent. Its mere jurisdictional presence engenders a universal regime that is able to reach into all family homes and at any time influence behaviours in the several ways reported. The 'no-fault' Family Law, in partnership with the threat of readily available restraining orders, can provide comfort for families, but only in normal behavioural circumstances. When the dark triad of hypergamy, Sociopathy, and mercenary syndrome is present, the two legal provisions can hover ominously over relevant family relationships like a constant sword of Damocles, to endanger the rights of trapped partners. No overt legal action is required to enable the coupled legal provisions to provide intrusive cover for blackmail, intimidation, and exploitation, as vividly brought to light in the preceding narrative.

The logical extension of this point has still worse ramifications. The behaviour of the wife in the investigated case revealed the 'no-fault' basis facilitated a Sociopathy-driven hypergamous, marry-for-money, mercenary syndrome that yielded a rags-to-riches reward of over a million dollars. The repugnance of that practice is aggravated when the Family Law's 'no-fault' basis collaterally encourages exploitation of moneyed Australian men for a scam-for-cash practice that, when cut to the chase, unveils the prevalence of the oldest profession with an unmentionable label. That would be so regardless of the merits of the Family Court judicial outcome. Only research can discover whether an indulgent 'no-fault' fostered underground industry of the depicted unseemly sort insidiously resides in Australia – an abuse that is bound to put Nigerian double-your-money scams well in the shade.

Adversarialism in Laxity

By looking searchingly at the illustrative case it was possible to hone in on two graceless pillars of the Family Court system. An unbridled adversarial system together with procedural laxity by design manifested institutional deficiency for behavioural impropriety.

Impunity for perjury arguably makes lying chic. Such exemption darkens the picture by motivating an embedded adversarial system to up the ante for disputants. One side feels free to vilify the other and is cordially detested in return. Truthfulness has become ever less relevant because verification has become ever less prevalent. The blossomed adversarial culture makes mutual ruthlessness from lies part and parcel of the process. In a family breakup situation featuring emotional trauma, the adversarial system adds fuel to the fire when beating each other up transforms heartache into rage. In the examined case, the more unethical sort of lawyers was found to be spoiling for a fight with tormenting perjurious abuse and weaponized discovery.

Faulty conduct is encouraged by slack court processes, all in the name of 'no-fault.' A genial environment for the unscrupulous was shown to enable Machiavellian gamesmanship for punishing the innocent wrongly accused of being at fault. When lax judicial processes are abused, as repeatedly happened in the analysed case, the resulting judicial dysfunction from permissiveness feeds upon itself from within, making it a conveniently indiscernible affliction that insidiously thrives. That implies administrative expediency trumps imperatives for justice as a matter of course.

The Family Court's adversarial environment whips up unsentimental compulsions. As a result, hotshot lawyers fired-up and craving professional success are compelled, more by necessity than choice, to batter the opposition and engage in unethical conduct. An adversarial court system featuring loose processes is too tempting not to claim the affection of lawyers lacking compunction. When process laxity attributable to 'no-fault' expands the ambit of discretion for lawyers, the permissiveness leaves room for the repertoire of questionable tactics and behaviours of the sort spotlighted in the examined case.

Be that as it may, it seems unfair to blame people for being creatures of their environment. The question arises whether all players in the court system (clients, lawyers, registrars, judges, and administrators), can be validly criticised for rational responses to distorted signals from a defective legal system. It may explain registrar behaviour that is cavalier, single-minded, and tunnel-visioned – all associated with lazy or expedient stereotypical rule-of-thumb solutions that smack of copout.

It appears that, at least for some lawyers, being down and dirty is necessary so that they can be up and running. The Family Court system is conducive to a cut-throat free-for-all race to the bottom, where is found the gutter. It should not therefore be surprising that, in the examined case, wife Mary's lawyers found their unethical approach to be driven more by necessity than choice. The system required them to join Mary in the gutter in order to successfully fight for her cause, which included making the mentally disabled homeless; they had to be in it to win it.

Into the bargain one can throw in the sordid abuse of the discovery process. What was reported offers a case study on the evil benefits of weaponising the discovery process for psychological warfare. In the examined case, the instrument of discovery was used to bludgeon the successful and hardworking husband Shaun by asking for voluminous information on 28 accounts and properties going back 22 years. But wife Mary was largely immune because she had underhandedly milked the relationship for years and so was left with next to nothing at the time of settlement. The contest was inherently uneven, but of no concern to the 'no-fault' Family Court.

Inexplicable Determinations

Appearances can be deceiving. Over 90 percent of cases resolve at the pre-trial stage, with only a fraction proceeding to a court trial. Does that seem like good news for the cause of justice or good news for the cause of expediency?

There is not enough information to determine whether judicial determinations at the pre-trial stage are reasonably reminiscent of the Wisdom of Solomon. What we do know is that, in the examined case, what was theoretically an innocuous recommendation by a registrar at the conciliation stage effectively became, due to the parties' poor health and advanced age, a directive that packed a deadly settle-or-else punch. As was painstakingly previously explained, the trappings of conciliation, supposedly a forum for voluntary agreement between the parties, can be window dressing for judicial decisions by registrars that smack of *fait accompli*.

Murkiness shakes confidence. The court system was shown to obscure the harmful effect of lax processes and questionable decisions from scrutiny – thereby giving the mislabelled 'no-fault' the bogus mantle of blamelessness. The absence of publicly documented justification for judicial determinations at the conciliation stage conceals their rationale. The outcome is effectively final for most and yet lacks transparency and accountability. That enables the Court's administrators to shrug off mistakes and hide skeletons in the Family Court's closet to sustain a spurious gloss on the process. Such opaqueness can enable failure to be mistaken for success.

Quick-fixes can deny justice because of 'no-fault' permissiveness. What happens at the pre-trail stage is a major determinant of overall

Family Court performance. Since reasons for determinations are not publicly recorded, a miscarriage of justice is a distinct possibility if the determination at conciliation is on a cavalier rule-of-thumb basis featuring the unthinkable: the disregarding of material facts. The scary possibility arises that informal approaches to life-changing decisions fostered by the 'no-fault' culture can open the door for the exercise of power without responsibility by registrars. The determinations made in such circumstances are more a threat than a triumph for justice when registrars fall short. Then, unsurprisingly, the sublime can go to the ridiculous.

But isn't there a fallback option? The question arises whether a bad pre-trial settlement can be avoided by appealing the matter and proceeding to a court trial. It was previously explained in some detail why rejecting the registrar's determination was dicey and best left to diehard sorts with bullfighter nerves who, moreover, had deep pockets with money to spare. For the vast majority of disputants, a court trial is shown to be a jittery prospect. A litigant's chances of winning as hoped for at the court trial were hypothesised to be not much different to a dart-throwing monkey's chances of hitting the target.

Taking a While

To top it all off there are notorious delays. Drawn out cases fatten files and weaken justice. Fat files obfuscating issues are incompatible with quick-fixes capable of real justice.

The slothful progress of cases is symptomatic of a congested court system. The weight of backlogged workload causes the wheels of justice to turn achingly slowly – generating money for lawyers to boot. Cases mired in unhappiness can take well over one year to sluggishly and painfully work their way through the pipeline till finally settled at the pre-trial stage. If the case is to reach trial it would take a ponderous 2-3 years longer, or still longer in tangled custody and financial cases.

Protraction crystallises exhaustion for disputants. They are worn down by months of fiendish investigation, confrontation, and expense. Lingering cases inflate legal fees to put lawyers in the pink and disputants in the dumps. The plodding disposition is antagonistic to the much-vaunted caring mission of the Family Court, as every day of delay dissipates resolve and involves pain for lives on hold, even as legal costs mount. Swelling costs promise a Spartan future for the large proportion of losing litigants.

12.3 Diagnosing 'No-fault'

Clinically diagnosing 'no-fault' helps one get to the bottom of the problem. Discovering the truth requires heaving 'no-fault' away from the realm of popular myth to uncover unpleasant facts. Revealed is that, over time, the 'no-fault' beating heart has become feeble, impaired by severe stresses from the adversarial system and process laxity. The 'no-fault' justice system operates in a dysfunctional way because sneakily evolving factors have weakened its original commendable function.

The examined case illustrated that the 'no-fault' basis is fuller of dreamy hope than proven success. Nevertheless it persists, perhaps only because inertia from blind faith in its original nobility obscures the current cold reality. Contrary to expectations, it is found to be expensive and nasty, not fine and dandy – a long way from being the best thing since sliced bread. It is small wonder that the singular 'no-fault' basis, which was spun as mantra for friendly caring, can be a recipe for sweeping unfairness.

But relapsing to the bad old days is hard to imagine. We should not be turning back the clock just because the promised salvation from the 'no-fault' basis is hard to find. The view of those who have a bad memory of the old 'fault' basis is bound to be: never again. To paraphrase Alex de Tocqueville (1805-1855): "The past no longer illuminates the future" and "the spirit walks in darkness" in the present. In other words, it cannot be said the 'no-fault' cure is worse than the bloodletting disease that it replaced. But that does not mean 'no-fault' has no faults that are all its own.

What society stands to gain from 'no-fault' is less clear than what it stands to lose; the pain from it is plain but the gain from it is veiled. In practice 'no-fault' has given rise to deficiencies that are insidious and entrenched, probably beneath the threshold of consciousness of some key Family Court players having a private stake in a public resource.

Analysing the illustrative case disclosed the nub of the problem. It was that justice can be subverted by the incompatibility of components operating within the Family Court system. In other words, interacting institutional segments that combine to make up the Family Court system – that is, its constituent elements – work at cross-purposes to degrade the Court's mission of caring justice. The virtuous 'no-fault' principle comes in a bundle accommodating grisly components that are inherently polarising, namely the adversarial system and process laxity. These auxiliary components are a barricade to 'no-fault' benefits; when they interact synergistically, the capability of 'no-fault' to deliver authentic justice is impeded.

That gives rise to the dire possibility that permissiveness resulting from synergy of the institutional mix can be so serious as to make the 'no-fault' based Family Court system a graveyard for justice.

Yet for all that, a requiem chorus for 'no-fault' justice would be unjustified; there is no conundrum. A way out of the impasse is explained shortly. The idea is to save what is left and regain what is lost. While it is a 'big ask' and requires taking the bit between one's teeth, it is a re-set that does not require going back to the drawing board. The to-be suggested reform promises to strike responsive chords because it has already shown it can be readily accommodated within the existing Family Court framework.

12.4 An Oddity

Cracks from the absence of procedural rigour cause the wellspring of justice to haemorrhage. That is because process laxity inherent in the indulgent 'no-fault' basis has the harmful effect of making propriety optional and misconduct fashionable in the several ways brought to light in the examined case. If lax processes, casual conciliation, and adversarialism are hallmarks of the Family Court system, in the examined case they were also the Achilles' heels of justice. Only research can reveal how often the drama in the Family Court theatre does really follow a socially honourable script.

Looking closer, the Family Court system seems to have evolved a long way from the noble hopes of its founders. As a result, it has in some ways become even worse than an ordinary court. If the Family Court has drifted away from its noble moorings of being a 'caring' court, yet does not have the rigour of an ordinary court, does not the information in *Family Court Perils* vividly illustrate that it falls between two stools? Brought out is that loose processes from absent robustness engenders a dark mood of distrust in those who know – *a la* Hirst in 'Kangaroo Court' previously cited. The evidence in this narrative supports Hirst's implication that achieving proper justice under the current system is a long shot. Hence, a sinking feeling is justified by the revelation that the current Family Court system is not all that it is cracked up to be. When expediency becomes respectable, the unimaginable becomes the norm.

The absence of procedural rigour creates a sinister setting for life-changing outcomes. The pathology of the Family Court system involves a damaging fusion of six elements: 'no-fault,' adversarial culture, process laxity, unpunished perjury, casual conciliation, and a lumbering pace. The factors converge synergistically to generate process abuse by unscrupulous disputants, leave room for lawyers to run amok, give the coercive advantage to the malicious, and enable incomprehensible decisions by registrars. The implication is that there is less than smooth sailing for cases battered by the perilous ill-winds from the toxic synergy.

Conflation of the six factors causes shoddiness. That comes from having more the trappings than substance of judicial processes worthy of a caring court. Hence the sobering question arises whether, on the basis of what is shown in the examined case, the Family Court system has evolved into something very different to that originally envisaged. The examined case strikingly illustrated the 'no-fault' Family Court system has lost its shine and is darkly uncanny. If the occurrences in the examined case are found to be examples of even fairly common happenings within the Family Court system, dismaying questions arise about the true state of health of that system. It may not be too far-fetched for the more cynical types to gain the impression that the Family Court system has mutated into some sort of a hideous medieval miscreation – to have regressed from the grandiose to the grotesque to have arguably become, in institutional terms, a judicial weirdo.

12.5 Reaching for a Star

For those who might have missed it, the aforementioned synergy explains why deficiencies in the Family Court system are much higher than they should be and justice is much weaker than it could be. That suggests six massive nails in the coffin of caring justice. And lying within it is the allegorical lady Justitia exhibiting dangerously infirm vital signs and close to breathing her last.

But singing a siren song in hyped praise of 'no-fault' is perfectly compatible with loud denunciation of it. That is because the fault with 'no-fault' is not in the concept of it but rather in the manner of its implementation; it is a good idea working badly (as palpably demonstrated by the case in point). For this reason, discarding the 'no-fault' principle, as some advocate, involves throwing the baby out with the bathwater. 'No-fault' is a necessary though insufficient condition for caring justice. Acknowledgement of that reality is the first step for dealing with the problem.

Reform is needed because the status quo, far from securing the future, jeopardizes it. There cannot be authentic justice without enough institutional rigour in the judicial system needed to deliver it. In the absence of reform addressing the core problems identified in this analysis, an entire area of law playing out on a vast stage would continue to be sweepingly dysfunctional. Unless reforms go beyond the peripheral to target the central, all the hot air generated by the dust-up among buttoned-down policy antagonists contesting control over policy would prove to be much ado about nothing much – implying a lipstick-on-pig outcome. For the 'no-fault' basis to regain its originally envisaged sparkle, reform needs to be more in the nature of root-and-branch as described next, than simply tinkering around the edges with band-aid solutions. That would avoid efforts that begin with hope from ending in farce.

We need to reach for a star that lies beyond the hangman's noose. What is called for is the transformation of current nightmarish visions into dreams of the future, while being mindful of their inherent susceptibility to naivety. For the Gordian knot to be cut, reforms would need to be driven by the following unshakable belief: process laxity inherent in the 'no-fault' basis makes an adversarial system repugnant and an inquisitorial system imperative.

Under an inquisitorial system, the court is actively involved in investigating the facts of the case by a single judge. That contrasts with an adversarial system, where the role of the court is primarily that of an impartial referee and more than one judicial officer may be sequentially involved in a single case – the latter risking exposure to 'reinventing-the-wheel' syndrome. Besides the horse sense in the proposition, the inquisitorial system has respectable templates in Scotland, Germany, Japan, among others. There is nothing offbeat about a non-adversarial judicial system even in Australia; there are examples of it already fitting within the framework of the existing Family Court system.

The changed theatre of action promises heartening benefits. When competent judges play an active role in taking charge of particular cases, two key triumphs emerge. One is that the scope for unethical moves by lawyers and clients is reduced; proceedings begin, not with malicious piffle in affidavits, but with the judge asking the parties to explain their position. The other is that the judge gets a pretty good feel for the case – a quantum leap forward from the current pre-trial situation – enabling better informed decisions. The examined case teaches the importance of judges being alert to personality disorders like Sociopathy, so they can have cognitive clarity for more insightful decisions. Obviously, in the reformed system, current practices like perjury and skulduggery would be *ipso facto* intolerable.

The scope for abuses reduces. Impairing the pole position for lawyers and registrars would minimise gaming of the system. Such pursuit is shown to have included craftily pulling the wool over registrars' eyes, using red herrings to draw registrars away from critical issues, making a drama of issues for unethical advantage, and inexplicable registrar determinations. Hence, the inquisitorial system would minimise inefficiencies from wasteful and vicious oppositional bun fights. And by giving the judicial reins to a properly qualified judge, reduce fiascos from registrar tails wagging judicial dogs.

We go back to the future. The proposed reform should restore what is lost, namely vigour to a faltering 'no-fault.' That should enable 'no-fault' to achieve its longed-for status as a properly functioning beating heart within a caring Family Court system. The change would incidentally, it is hoped, bring the presently unleashed permissiveness-genie under control, if not put back in the bottle.

12.6 Future Prospects

But the desired regeneration is more a hope than an expectation. In all probability it is a while off because there appear to be far more people devoted to the status quo than there are questioning it.

There is no painless way to change the catalytic spin-off effects of the current easygoing 'no-fault' arrangement. Change is forestalled by the adversarial system being etched in as conventional wisdom, and for that reason regarded as the natural order of things. That empowers the legal profession, as a lionized vested interest, to entrench the status quo. It becomes a roadblock to reform when ending their romance with belligerency is difficult for lawyers regarding it as an income-generating normalcy. Lawyers can be expected to come out swinging, far from cheerful about threats to fizz in fee-generation.

For the above reasons, the adversarial system can inspire affection from the entrenched such that it feeds upon itself for the doom loop of self-perpetuation. If that be the case, the chance of a full-fledged inquisitorial system happening anytime soon is as low as a summer snowfall.

Out of the woodwork of the foregoing analysis emerges a choice of conclusions. Take one's pick depending on whether one sees the glass as half empty or half full. For the 'half full' dreamy optimistic bunch, the conclusion is that 'hope springs eternal;' for the 'half empty' realistic pessimistic bunch, the conclusion is 'don't hold your breath.'

***

References

REFERENCES

Festinger, Leon (1957), *A Theory of Cognitive Dissonance*, Stanford University Press, California.

Hirst, John (2005), 'Kangaroo Court' *Quarterly Essay*, Issue 17, Australia.

Stout, Martha (2005) *The Sociopath Next Door*, Harmony Books, New York.

White, Alasdair (2009) *From Comfort Zone to Performance Management*, ISBN 978-2-930583, White & Maclean Publishing. Hoeilaart, Belgium

***